CHILDREN
OF A
LESSER GOD

MARK MEDOFF

AMBER LANE PRESS

First published in 1980 by
James T. White & Company, Clifton, New Jersey, U.S.A.

This edition first published 1982,
reprinted 1983, 1985, 1989, 1993, 1996 by
Amber Lane Press Ltd,
Church Street, Charlbury, Oxford OX7 3PR
Telephone and fax: 01608 810024

Printed and bound by Guernsey Press Co. Ltd, Guernsey, C.I.

ISBN 0 906399 32 7

CHILDREN
OF A
LESSER GOD

For why is all around us here
As if some lesser god had made the world,
But had not force to shape it as he would?

"Idylls of the King"
Tennyson

For
PHYLLIS FRELICH and BOB STEINBERG
who gave everything to it

Originally produced on Broadway by
Emanuel Azenberg, The Shubert Organization,
Dasha Epstein and Ron Dante

Originally Produced by
Center Theatre Group of Los Angeles
at the Mark Taper Forum

NOT SO RANDOM NOTES
FROM THE PLAYWRIGHT

It seems, *finally, to be about family.*

In January, 1977, I am in Rhode Island doing a workshop of a new play called *The Conversion of Aaron Weiss.* I have known the scenic and lighting designer Bob Steinberg for a year. He has done a lighting design for me a year before and is doing the set and lights for this production at the University of Rhode Island, where he is a member of the faculty. I am vaguely aware that, though a hearing person, he was in on the beginnings of the National Theatre for the Deaf; that he fell in love with one of NTD's actresses, Phyllis Frelich, deaf from birth. I know Phyllis "retired" when they married and moved into the countryside of Rhode Island. I know they have two sons; Phyllis, they say, is busy being a mother and homemaker but, boy, I should have seen her when she was an actress!

I am told that I will find Phyllis Frelich irresistible; everyone does. I prep myself to resist. *She's probably not that hot—deaf woman, handicapped, people feel sorry for her—overcompensate in praise. I won't fall for that.*

Our first "conversation": I do not realize I am speaking loudly—as if she might hear if I get the decibel level up high enough. I also mouth my syllables carefully: *Hel-lo, Phyl-lis, I am so hap-py to meet you.* I am uninformed enough to think that all deaf people read lips. Many don't, Phyllis Frelich among them. (She comes from a family of eight deaf siblings, deaf parents. American Sign Language is their means of speaking; to them we're the ones who are handicapped.)

I learn quickly that I don't know very damn much about deaf people. My experience runs to coughing up quarters in shopping centers for those little manual alphabet cards and somehow lumping the deaf all together with Patty Duke (a hearing actor) as Helen Keller in *The Miracle Worker.* Not exactly a comprehensive knowledge of the subject.

Bob has to translate in order for Phyllis and me to talk. I immediately make another common mistake: I speak to *him* instead of her, as if she were in another country and he were some telephonic conduit. I am reminded of the cowboy and Indian movies of my childhood: *Tell Red Cloud me want be him friend.*

By the end of the second "conversation," by which time I have learned how to sign *How are you? I am fine*—not exactly "communication" but I feel very frisky—I tell her I'll write a play for her.

Why? Because she's a pitiable deaf lady? Because I want to "save" the deaf and earn the undying gratitude of one of the last available

vi

minorities? No. Because she points out to me that there are no parts in the canon of "hearing" theatre for deaf actors and because the two of them—Phyllis *and* Bob—are separately and together ... well: irresistible. Honest people, fiercely full of life and love, and as open as any two people I've met.

They think it's a nice gesture—*He says he's going to write a play for you*—but know it's just idle talk, the result of fascination, pleasant companionship, and a few drinks.

When I become chairman of the Drama Department at New Mexico State University in July of 1978 I have it in my head that I want to develop an undergraduate theatre program that has a small permanent faculty supplemented by visiting professionals. I ask for a lot of money so I can pay these professionals small amounts and bring a lot of them in. I start by preying on friends. The first are Frelich and Steinberg. I tell them if they'll come in January of 1979, I'll have the supposed play I'm going to write for Phyllis ready to go into rehearsal.

As much as I relish one-on-one athletic competition, I have nevertheless relished equally the interdependence, the sharing, the collaboration, the *familial* nature of team sports. Work in the theatre on a play by a group of people has about it those qualities. For the most part, we leave the worst of ourselves outside the theatre and bring the best inside.

The Medoffs, the Steinbergs, the faculty and students of the Drama Department of New Mexico State University spend five months virtually living together as we work on a script that is being born day to day. I write in the mornings, Phyllis and Bob and I work in the afternoons, the company rehearses in the evenings. We build, change, learn. The learning promotes more building and changing.

Bob is not merely the interpreter any longer. He is playing James Leeds and to my eye, like Phyllis, thriving. He has an honesty that comes off the stage exactly as it resides in him.

I run characters in and out of the script like a football coach trying out rookies in training camp. I will not soon forget Ernie Putnam, the "nice" hearing boy in Sarah's adolescence, who is with us for weeks. He wants to marry Sarah, but Sarah's sister Ruth, a character who survives the first production, steals him away. Then, too, there is Sarah's father, who makes an appearance for several days. I still remember his bittersweet scene with Sarah fondly.

Though it is Sarah who most interests me, the play is more about James. Why? It'll take me months to admit the reason; it won't happen until I begin to work with Gordon Davidson. But it's because I'm not secure enough as a "deaf person" myself to write the play I want to write, the one in which James and Sarah share the stage equally. Face it—like many male writers throughout history, I am accustomed to focussing on the male protagonist and surrounding him with functional females. I've been telling myself for years I really ought to stop doing that. The thing is, it's not that easy.

By the time we show the play for four performances in Las Cruces in April, we know—despite the incompleteness of the script—that we are in the midst of creating something special.

My agent Gilbert Parker comes out. He has always been an accurate barometer of the quality and producibility of my work. For the first time since he read *The Wager,* he's really excited by one of my plays.

Gilbert sends the play out in June to five theatres. Seasons are pretty well set by now. Two theatres want to consider it for *next* season. One thinks the play will offend deaf people. (Quite a mind at work there!) The Papp people will get to reading it "soon." Gordon Davidson is interested and happens to find himself suddenly with a hole in his season; the Mark Taper Forum has scheduled *Strider, The Story of a Horse* in its second slot, to follow the west coast premieres of Lanford Wilson's *Talley's Folly* and *The Fifth of July* in repertory. The rights to *Strider,* however, are unavailable.

I know Gordon from 1973 when he included my play *The Kramer* in the New Theatre for Now Festival of that year. He is someone I've wanted to work with since.

He askes me to come to L.A. to discuss the possibility of doing the play.

I arrive by cab at his house in Santa Monica early one morning in the middle of August, almost a year ago to the day as I write; and, if one were into omens, how about these: We embrace. Gordon suggests we go out to his study, which is off the pool. The phone rings. He answers. I wait anxiously. (The first meeting of a writer and a director is like nothing so much as a mail order marriage) He hangs up. Gets up. We head for the door. The phone rings. He answers it. I check out *Theatre World 78-79,* see how many times I'm listed. *Once.* I experience a moment of desperate desire for the success of this play. I want Gordon and me to want to work together. Yet, we're off to a stinking start: I am less important than these phone calls. He hangs up. Gets up. The phone rings. It's for his wife Judi. The tide could be turning. We go outside. The study is in sight, the commencement of vows only a short flight of steps away. Men are working around the Davidson pool, laying tile. As we pass—as we are *about* to pass—one of the men knocks a yard or so of concrete *into* the pool. The cement sinks and spreads through the water; the automatic pool cleaner goes after the viscid, lumpy glob. Good luck.

Gordon has a remarkable temperament; it is something I will come to admire in the next months, though never so much as at that moment: Your standard homeowner—me, for instance—would scream, would rant and rage at someone who knocks concrete into his swimming pool. But it's done and no one is more unhappy about it than the workman himself. So why bother? Gordon Davidson doesn't.

We go to his study where the phone is ringing. He answers. I select a seat and look around at the memorabilia of the man's theatre life: posters and set designs from plays he shepherded to completion: *The Trial of the Catonsville Nine, In the Matter of J. Robert Oppenheimer, The Shadow Box* ... He hangs up. And after what seems an entire business day, we start to talk. No. We start thrashing about with brains and tongues for a language with which we may eventually start to talk. A great deal could be written about the relationship of playwrights and their directors. Suffice it to say that ultimately they must be symbiotic and will succeed or fail by virtue of their communication techniques.

We do not communicate well that first day. Yet, when Gordon assures me that the Taper's doing *Children* doesn't depend on his directing it—that I can direct it myself—something urges me to say unequivocally: *No, I want you to direct it.*

In my life's history to date, no decision I've made strikes me as any wiser.

Most people haven't the faintest notion what the new play process is about, haven't the remotest idea what part a director can—and should—play in the development of a new play.

Gordon is the most remarkable director I've worked with in terms of getting into my head, seeking the light at the end of the labyrinth, and driving me toward it through a hundred or two false and true turns.

Not that I always appreciate his methods. For weeks, it seems he manages not a kind word about my work on the play, only that he wonders about this, doesn't think that works, wishes I'd look again at this *and* that. And yet I am aware that I am being challenged to go beyond where I've been before and assured that, despite the current tensions of the trip, I'll have his unwavering support. I am, he seems to say, as much a competitor as you. So let's go.

In the last weeks in August, we meet in New York. Phyllis and Bob have been wandering around the country wondering *if* the play will be done this season, and if so, *where*. They audition for Gordon, do very nice work for him. It is likely, though, that a more experienced actor than Bob will play James; it is a likelihood that is difficult to adjust to. Only Bob (on stage) and I (in my head) have been James for as long as there has been a James, and though not a schooled actor, Bob has brought the part an unimpeachable truthfulness. And beyond that, there is the bond among the two of them, me, and this play. Bob envisions being surgically excised from the body whole; it is an unenviable position, one which he will occupy with more dignity over the next months than I imagine possible.

Gordon and I meet again in L.A., where we read the play—beginning to change now as a result of our developing ability to speak a common language to each other.

It is at this time I meet for the first time a young actor named John Rubinstein in a small hotel room in Beverly Hills (Yes, there *are* small hotel rooms in Beverly Hills). My first impression is that he seems absolutely right for James Leeds. Little do I know then that he will be absolutely right for *each* of the several metamorphoses James Leeds goes through in the next months, that he will change like a chameleon as fast as I alter his environment and that he will thrive with the challenge.

It is after this second visit to Los Angeles that I return home to Las Cruces and, en route, decide to cut six characters out of the play ten days before rehearsals are to begin and to write a completely new second act. Though it has been Gordon's encouragement that has pushed me to look anew at the script and has now led me to scuttle all but the characters absolutely necessary to James and Sarah's story, he is *very* silent (a redundancy, I know) for quite a while on the phone when I announce this momentous decision to him.

"In other words," he says, "I should stop auditioning people for those roles."

My wife Stephanie and I pack up the kids and head for L.A. Rent a house with a private beach in Malibu. Often these temporary relocations are met by the family with moderated, let us say, constrained enthusiasm. Not this time. I often wish I could be there to enjoy the house, the beach, the sound of the waves. I leave the house at ten in the morning, return anytime from dinner time to one a.m. The twice daily drive along the Coast Highway, though, is strangely mollifying, some compensation when I think how many times I've driven from Las Cruces to the El Paso Airport and back and wished only that the car could take wing. Between Malibu and Santa Monica (where I hit the freeway and the traffic of legend) I tend to feel, as they say, *laid back*.

I spend the first week of rehearsals locked in the production stage manager's office at the rear of the Taper while the company rehearses or discusses or chews up the pages coming off my borrowed typewriter. (I imagine that I am being tested for qualification in some licensing procedure anytime this rehearsal process begins: *All right, Mr. Medoff, now what do you do when both engines conk out at thirty-five thousand feet and you've left your parachute in the trunk with your last play?)* Though I often slosh around in self-pity, insisting if someone doesn't come to my garret and say a kind word to me about the rewrites I'll explode in authorly fury, no one does and I continue to try to find my way through the corridors of the maze.

As with any new play in rehearsal, there is a lot of advice coming my way. Given my increasing trust in Gordon, I ask him to collect advice and assail me with expurgated lists. He writes down in outline form over and over where he thinks I'm trying to go. He talks "focus" to me; I am currently into shotgun fire, spraying buckshot at a big space; he's trying to get me to switch, say, to a nice big game rifle with a good scope on it. By the second week of rehearsal we both think we have agreed where we think I'm trying to go. I finish a new second act. I'm very excited about it. I ask Bob to take a sneak preview the second Sunday morning while the rest of the company works on the first act. I leave him alone to read it, and plague myself as follows: *He has to weep at the end or it's not even close yet.* When I return to the office, I find him weeping.

We read the new second act in rehearsal that afternoon. Everyone is pleased. (And relieved. We open in two weeks. Be nice to have a few days to *rehearse* the second act. Be even nicer to give John Rubinstein, the fastest sign language learner anyone has ever seen, time to learn to *sign* James' abundance of lines.)

A funny thing is happening to me; I am feeling like a nicer human being; I am writing more humanely. I'm aware of feeling rather obsessed with Stephanie and the children, with the warmth, the ... necessity of the family. I feel differently than I have before about the characters I'm writing. For the first time in my writing career I want to create fully sympathetic characters. Some part of me has heretofore hated something in my characters (me, no doubt) and conveyed that unsympathetic quality onto the stage: *Here, audience, now you like these people in spite of the fact you don't want to. Go on or I'll write even nastier people next time!*

This change in my work comes, I think, from the family, yes, but also from the particular associations I've had during the writing of this play. The company at New Mexico State University and, even more palpably, the association with Phyllis and Bob, Gordon and John, and the company and staff of the Mark Taper Forum. I have never had much respect for the nature of most humans. Suddenly I am awash in it and trying to write characters with a humanity equal to that of the people portraying and helping me to complete them. These are landmark associations, no matter what the reception of this play, and I find myself looking forward hungrily to further theatrical expressions of these new feelings.

We are quite a hit in L.A. Audiences laugh and cry. They like these people and are moved by their lives. They are also conscious, I think, of being present at the birth of a historical undertaking. Though I never sat around and wondered what hadn't been done before, certainly I am mindful of the "newness" of this play's concept, and Gordon has all along urged me to find the essential moments, scenes, ideas that make the relationship of James and Sarah unique.

We have all dreamed aloud, if with caution, about opening, being big, and then entertaining a shuttle of New York producers.

In fact, they come in large numbers and we can choose among them. *Manny Azenberg and the Shubert Organization, Dasha Epstein and Ron Dante, we select you. To move us to New York. To Broadway.*

Well, let's not kid around: Thoughts of Broadway are as frightening as they are titillating. A play about a deaf broad and a hearing guy on Broadway? The Great White Way? *The Street?* For four hundred thousand dollars! It's one thing to be credible in L.A. at the Taper where Gordon has accustomed his audience to unusual and often extraordinary *but* uncommercial fare. But Broadway, home of the comedy, the musical, and the musical comedy? A place that seems to accord only an obligatory straight play or two a year the honor of opening and then being roundly ignored by a public that doesn't want to pay through the nose to meet in the theatre the sort of reality it meets outside.

And forget all that—there's still trouble in the second act. A debate ensues concerning the political nature of the second act. Should I get rid of the politics? Should I expand the first act and make the whole play the journey *to* the marriage?

I rewrite back in Las Cruces. I send pages to L.A. Gordon and I talk. I find I am wed to the political nature of the second act. I stop caring what anyone else thinks. Gordon, though he has reservations, goes along with me. Though I know enough to continue to listen and sift advice, I'm very tired of it. I want to be through with this play and on to something else. It's a solid year of working with others—beloved though they are—day to day. It is the lack of time to be truly alone with the muse, as much as anything, that is becoming progressively more disquieting.

Phyllis and John and Gordon and I rehearse for a week after Christmas in L.A. Sarah is becoming stronger, more equal to James. Now when I rewrite I find myself (finally) automatically seeing the play from her point of view. The music scene evolves in one long day of rehearsal when I go to and from typewriter and rehearsal hall several times and behave rather badly at one point when I think if Gordon or John asks me to rearrange or rewrite it once more I'll behave in a manner even *more* juvenile. I survive the day, aware we've created a terrific scene in the best collaborative tradition of the theatre. (I am amazed at John's ability, unlike most actors, to truly maintain an overview of the entire play rather than to see the whole entirely from his character's point of view.)

Gordon and I speculate and conjecture about how we'll be received in New York. We are guarded in our optimism. Or is it a sham? On my part anyway. In fact, am I not fiercely confident that we'll *fly*? Truth to tell, yes I am. I sense Gordon is. Yet, he speaks often of how well *Zoot Suit* was received last season at the Taper and of the disaster in New York.

Bob, meanwhile, is in New York looking for a place to live. Phyllis and I spend the free time of these days alone. I love not having an interpreter available so I have to do all my own signing. Over a Chinese dinner one night—when the two of us eat eight dishes, seconds on rice, and two pots of tea—each admits to the other that he believes his world is about to alter greatly by virtue of our move to New York.

The *esprit* within the company in New York is ... what? Modestly defiant. We look down from the forty-fifth floor of the Minskoff Building where we rehearse; visible far below is the street we hope to conquer. From this height it looks not only unthreatening but practically defenseless.

Never mind that, on the financial side—and it's not all Art for Art's sake, you know—we have an advance sale of $22.50. That's one orchestra ticket on the weekend. Yet, no one is worried, or at least not doing any worrying out where we can watch it. Not even producer Manny. Gutsy guy Manny. I really believe his faith in us is genuine, even though the advertising campaign he's running is somewhere between nonexistent and very low-key. *An extraordinary love story.* What a line! *Sshh, sshh, sshh,* he says. *Relax. Let people discover us,* he says, *let the critics discover us. Trust me,* he says. The funny thing is, I do. (Months later I find out why when I play my one and only game with the company softball team in the Broadway Show League: He's a damn good outfielder; together we spend several happy hours roaming the outfield pasture of Central Park, gamboling like two colts. It's a good thing we didn't know back in early March when we were rehearsing that the team would win one game and lose the other fifteen or twenty. That modest defiance might have been something more akin to catatonic terror.)

On my fortieth birthday, I am in New York City. Stephanie and the girls are still at home in Las Cruces. I call from the pay phone backstage at the Longacre, accept Happy Birthday wishes in a gentlemanly fashion. Then Stephanie informs me that our oldest daughter, Debra, age eleven, is going that night to her first boy-girl party. Ever. I contemplate suicide.

Thirteen nights later, opening night on Broadway, I will wonder if I wasn't a hair too hasty foregoing suicide on my fortieth.

Opening night is a major disappointment. The Daily News reviewer, a person who truly ought to be in another line of work, jabbers on in his defensive—and always in the case of my work—vitriolic prose about a play quite different from the one we think we performed. (Of course, you've heard *that* one before from righteous playwrights.) Walter Kerr of *The Times* writes what many insist is a "good" review; it is, to my eye—however "good"—pretty bad. No one is going to rush out to see the play he reviewed. The television reviews are very good. None, however, meets us with the impassioned admiration I have fantasized in *my* versions of their reviews.

I am not in a good mood. Phyllis and Bob, Bill and Liz Frankfather (Bill plays Mr. Franklin and was in the very first production of *The Wager* in 1967), Stephanie and I do not drink a bottle of wine Bill has kept and carried since the beginning of rehearsals in L.A. eight months earlier. I go to bed anticipating we'll close within a few weeks.

You would think I would lie awake and agonize all night. But I'm too tired. The morning and the days to come will be time enough for self-pity and recriminations.

It's raining the next morning. Perfect: I hate rain. I go into Central Park to run. I conjure up a scenario in which I die grotesquely (though instantly) in front of a bus. Walter Kerr will lament not having written a better "good" review. The fellow from the Daily News will assess his integrity, find it wanting, and move to a small New England village, there to become an electrician's apprentice, only to electrocute himself through sheer incompetence.

There are, however, no buses in the park. At least not where I run. I'm forty now. Maybe I'll have a heart attack or a stroke. Instead, I promote my good health with a splash around the reservoir and return to the hotel full of brave thoughts, more or less game to face the traditional morning-after-opening-night conclave. The writer, his agent, the producers, the ad agency people meet to plot the future of the play.

I anticipate a wake, a lot of glances deflected from my face, some sympathetic hands on my shoulder, talk of "getting them next time." It is still raining and we do not have an umbrella. Contemptuously, I refuse to buy one. Stephanie is unwilling to point out to me this particular morning—as if I don't know—how stupid that is. She is equally unwilling, however, to get drenched with me and runs from the cab to the building under Gordon's umbrella.

Upstairs, instead of gloom, I find calm determination. The producers promise that the play will run through the Tony Awards, even if they have to put another hundred and fifty thousand into it. I am moved by these people's generosity and continuing faith that this play will make it. And if it doesn't, it will at least run close to one hundred performances; I can round it off, tell people: *Oh sure, it ran a hundred performances.* Not humiliating, anyway.

And then Clive Barnes' review comes in in the afternoon *Post.* Bill Raidy in the Newhouse chain. Jacques LeSourd in the Gannett chain. Radio reviews. Hints of the Newsweek review. The AP and UPI. And they are, at best, love letters, at worst, damn good.

I begin to wish I had bought an umbrella. I feel the onset of pneumonia. I don't want to die—that was only kidding around. As if to cap the new optimism, Bernie Jacobs (one of the Shuberts) assures us one and all that the threatened transit strike, set to hit the subways, trains and buses at midnight that night will be averted and we won't have *that* to contend with on top of a $22.50 advance sale and a "good" review in *The Times.*

I am a touch miffed when that night, at midnight, the transit workers walk out. Is the upswing to be *that* short?

The next day the future begins to divulge its shape. Get this: People *walk* to see *Children of a Lesser God.* We almost break even that first week. We do the second week. We continue upward until we are, at this writing, playing to capacity.

So, we're a big hit. What to worry about now? Why, the Pulitzer Prize, of course. The New York Drama Critics Circle Award. The Outer Critics Circle Award. The Drama Desk Award.

And, oh yeah, the Tony.

And now the obligatory disclaimer concerning awards in the arts: It *is* ludicrous to judge among other works of art *the best* since the better ones tend to be qualitatively similar and otherwise dissimiliar, invested with the peculiarities of their creators. *But,* if there are going to be *best* awards, I'd a helluva lot rather win them than lose them to someone else.

The word among the cognoscenti is that this is Lanford Wilson's year, that *Talley's Folly* will sweep the hardware. I try to accept this like a good sport. I succeed well enough so that when, indeed, we do not get the Pulitzer and the New York Drama Critics Circle Award, I am only disappointed.

Stephanie and Manny are not only disappointed, they are furious. They are both bad sports. Frankfather is wondering if I want to go with him to injure some people. He is a good person to go with; he is 6'5", 225. I explain to him that I can't because I am busy preparing to lose the Tony, as are John (who expects to lose to Judd Hirsch of *Talley's Folly*) and Gordon (who expects to lose to Vivian Matalon, director of the revival of *Mornings at Seven*) and Phyllis (who is afraid to believe us when we tell her she'll win).

And then we win the Outer Critics Circle and Drama Desk Awards. And in some distant secret place, I decide we might win the Tony for Best Play and six nights before the Awards, I get out of bed at eleven o'clock, stand in front of the mirror, and start to practice an acceptance speech.

The word on the Street when Stephanie and I arrive in New York is that it's a toss-up between Lanford and me, that Ann Twomey is pushing Phyllis, and that John and Gordon are out of the running.

John assures me we are going to lose all four, that we *must* all keep our hopes down. Protect ourselves! Keep our defenses *up*! I know he's offering sensible advice but it's too late for me. I am no longer prepared to lose. Everything in me wants to win. If I lose, I am going to have to suffer what I suppose will amount to the greatest disappointment in my life.

As on opening night in L.A., as on opening night in New York, I am completely sober Tony night. Tough guy? No. I just want to record for posterity with my own mind's eye what happens to me tonight and how I behave in the face of it.

Stephanie and I come to the Mark Hellinger Theatre with Phyllis and Bob in a limousine. We keep touching each other, as if proximity alone is not enough. When we unload from our limo, no one knows us. I am conscious of thinking we should hurry inside so that our car can pull away and the car of someone the throngs *will* recognize can pull up and unload.

I am nervous until we enter the theatre. Then, there among so many others wanting the award as much as I, I am suddenly calm, almost euphoric, as if I had been writing for several hours or running for several miles.

We separate, Phyllis and Bob going to one aisle, Stephanie and I to another. John is just down and across the aisle from us, Gordon further down and off to John's side. Lanford is directly across from me.

We hope that if nothing else, we get on camera in some shot or other so our children and friends in Las Cruces can see us. We clamp our hands together and try to pay attention to the pre-show instructions concerning the behavior of winners. (How 'bout some pointers on how to lose?)

When Vivian Matalon gets the Tony for Best Director I want so badly for Gordon, I assume everything is running true to the Street word (and to the Rubinstein word, as so far John's right—we're losing everything).

When the Best Actor winner is named, however, I find I'm not the least bit surprised to hear that his name is John Rubinstein. And it crosses my mind as my mouth babbles over and over again, "Oh Johnny, oh Johnny ..." that we're going to go right on and sweep the remaining awards.

When Phyllis wins, though, my emotion is momentarily tainted by a fear that, like Gordon, I'll lose, that the director and the writer will appear to be honorable only because of two great performances. But then, with Bob interpreting beside her, Phyllis Frelich stands before her colleagues, before thirty million television viewers—this woman I love, who is like a sister to me, whose radiance and talent dazzle me—and I am moved past love to wonder at what we have done to each other's lives.

Then James Earl Jones announces the award for Best Play. And I am in flight from my wife's embrace to that stage still.

August 16, 1980
Las Cruces, NM

Children of a Lesser God was first performed on April 25, 1979 in a workshop production at New Mexico State University. It was presented by the Center Theatre Group at the Mark Taper Forum in Los Angeles from October 25 – December 9, 1979. The play opened in New York on March 30, 1980 at the Longacre Theatre.

The first London production of *Children of a Lesser God* was at the Mermaid Theatre on August 25, 1981. The cast was as follows:

SARAH NORMAN:	Elizabeth Quinn
JAMES LEEDS:	Trevor Eve
ORIN DENNIS:	Ed Kelly
MR FRANKLIN:	John Graham
MRS NORMAN:	Irene Sutcliffe
LYDIA:	Julianne Gold
EDNA KLEIN:	Joan Blackham

Directed by Gordon Davidson

The play transferred to the Albery Theatre, London, on October 6, 1981.

THE CHARACTERS

JAMES LEEDS:	*thirty-ish. A speech teacher at a State School for the Deaf.*
SARAH NORMAN:	*mid-twenties. Deaf from birth.*
ORIN DENNIS:	*in his twenties. Has some residual hearing; a lip reader.*
MRS. NORMAN:	*Sarah's mother.*
MR. FRANKLIN:	*anywhere from his early thirties to his mid-forties. The Supervising Teacher at the Deaf School.*
LYDIA:	*in her late teens. Has some residual hearing; a lip reader.*
EDNA KLEIN:	*thirty to forty. A lawyer.*

The play takes place in the mind of James Leeds. Throughout the events, characters step from his memory for anything from a full scene to several lines.

The stage is bare, holding only a few benches and a blackboard and permitting characters to appear and disappear easily.

As to the matter of Signed English. When James is speaking to Sarah, who is deaf and does *NOT* lip read, he signs what he says to her unless otherwise noted. When speaking to Orin and Lydia, who both lip read, he merely speaks directly into their faces and enunciates with some care.

Sarah speaks aloud only at the end of the play. Otherwise the notion of speech where she is concerned means strictly the use of Signed English or American Sign Language (ASL). The difference between ASL and Signed English basically is that the former is far more conceptual and pictorial than grammatical, Signed English employing a word-by-word technique.

[Brackets] indicate portions of a line which are signed but not spoken.

ACT ONE

James and Sarah alone, met at the climax of an argument they'll replay at the end of the play. She "speaks" here in ASL; were we to translate it into standard English, she would be saying: *I have nothing; no hearing, no speech, no intelligence, no language. I have only you. I don't need you. I have me alone. Join, unjoined.*

SARAH: Me have nothing. Me deafy. Speech inept. Intelligence —tiny blockhead. English—blow away. Left one you. Depend—no. Think myself enough. Join, unjoined—

(Sarah runs off)

JAMES: *(Not signing)* She went away from me. Or did I drive her away? I don't know. If I did, it was because ... I seem to be having trouble stringing together a complete ... I mean, a speech therapist shouldn't be having difficulty with the language. All right, start in the ... *Finish the sentence!* Start in the beginning. In the beginning there was silence and out of that silence there could come only one thing: Speech. That's right. Human speech. So, *speak!*

(Orin has entered the classroom area—looks at the blackboard on which is written the following:)

ORIN: "Speech is not a specious but a sacred sanctio*na*, secured by solemn sacrifice."

JAMES: *(A together, energetic James)* Very good, Orin.

ORIN: No, it wasn't.

1

JAMES: It was better. A couple of things, though—

ORIN: Mr. Leeds, remember you have to look at me when you're talking.

JAMES: Sorry. A couple of things though. Specious. Specious. It's softer, like sshhh.

ORIN: Specious.

JAMES: All right, good. And the final "n" in sanction.

ORIN: Sanctio*na*.

JAMES: Wait, please. Watch. Sanctio*n*. Un. Un.

ORIN: Sanctio*na*. That was wrong, damn it!

JAMES: That's okay, Orin ... Watch my mouth. Cut it. Sanctio*n*. Look up in here. Sanctio*n*. "Un." *(Indicating the movement of the tongue to the roof of the mouth)*

ORIN: Sanctio*n*.

JAMES: Yes! Good for you. How did that feel?

ORIN: How did it sound?

JAMES: It sounded beautiful.

ORIN: Then it felt all right.

JAMES: Speech.

ORIN: Speech.

(Franklin and Sarah enter)

FRANKLIN: Mr. Leeds ...

JAMES: *(Indicating that Franklin should wait; keeping his focus on Orin)* Specious.

ORIN: Specious.

JAMES: Sanction.

ORIN: Sanctio*na*.

JAMES: No ...

ORIN: Sanction.

JAMES: Yes. Hello, Mr. Franklin. How are you, sir?

FRANKLIN: Just dandy, Mr. Leeds. That was very impressive, Orin.

ORIN: Thank you, Mr. Franklin.

2

FRANKLIN: You never worked that hard for me.

ORIN: *(Signing and speaking—the signing for Sarah's benefit)*
I never liked you, Mr. Franklin. [Asshole.]

FRANKLIN: Ah. No garlic then for Mr. Leeds—or is two weeks
too soon to decide the garlic question?

ORIN: You want to smell?

FRANKLIN: No thanks. I just had an ice cream cone.

JAMES: *(Smoothing things)* Orin, I think that'll be all for today.

ORIN: Could I see you tomorrow maybe?

JAMES: Sure, you want to have lunch with me?

ORIN: Okay. Thank you.

SARAH: *(As Orin greets her and is about to pass)* Ass licker.	JAMES: *(To Franklin as Orin moves away)* Garlic?
ORIN: *(Signing only)* [Think so? Bend over and find out.]	FRANKLIN: Sometimes they like to chew a little garlic for the speech therapist.

(She does; Orin smiles and passes her)

SARAH: Chicken.

ORIN: *(Signing only)* [Later.]

(Orin leaves)

FRANKLIN: *(Signing the following dialogue)* Mr. Leeds, this is
Sarah.

JAMES: Hello, Sarah.

FRANKLIN: Say hello to Mr. Leeds, Sarah.

SARAH: You deaf?

JAMES: Am I deaf? No. Why?

(She looks as if she may exit)

FRANKLIN: Stay!

(She imitates a dog "staying")

Cute.

JAMES: Well, you did say that to her as if—

FRANKLIN: *(No longer signing)* Pardon me, Mr. Leeds, but save the lectures for staff meeting, okay? Sarah has a certain aversion to learning speech, but she worked so hard for your predecessor that I can't imagine she won't do the same for you. So, I'd like you to take Sarah on in your spare time.

JAMES: *(A bit intimidated by her)* Well, I wouldn't go so far as to say I *have* any spare—

(Franklin thrusts Sarah's file toward James, ending the discussion. James takes it)

Fine.

FRANKLIN: Good. Do you play bridge?

JAMES: Yes, I do.

FRANKLIN: Good. Eight o'clock tonight, my place. *(To Sarah)* Deaf power. Thumb up.

(Franklin goes. James speaks to Sarah as if he assumes she can lip read)

JAMES: Well, Sarah. Would you like to sit down? Right here.

(He sits. She remains standing)

Okay, why don't we both stand then?

(He stands. She sits)

I see. Very good. You got me there.

(He sits. She is inattentive)

Could you look at me, please. Excuse me, if you don't look at me, I can't ...

4

(She looks at him)

So. You are one of the dorm assistants, is that correct? Or an apprentice instructor?

(She stares curiously at his mouth)

Ah—no, I see it says right here you're a maid. A maid?

(She stares at his mouth)

I can't help detecting a certain reluctance to communicate with me. Is that because you're afraid you'll be embarrassed by the sounds you make?

(She stares at his mouth)

Are you reading my lips? I don't think you're reading my lips. *(Signing)* Gee, that was quick of me. Okay ...

(He loosens up his fingers and wrists and begins to sign)

Why don't we start by signing with each other and maybe for next week we can shoot for an oral interpretation of F-i-n-n—

(Stops spelling—he mouths it carefully)

Finnegan's Wake? Forget it, bad joke. Want to play stand up, sit down again?

(He's bombing)

Gee, this is nice. I get the feeling Mr. Franklin is trying to play a little joke on the new teacher—putting his ... *(Speaking it only)* ... delusions of grandeur—*(Signing)* —how do you sign delusions—e-l-u-s-i-o-n-s—"dream"? *(Nothing)* You know, the joke would be on Franklin if I just came in here and got you to speak for me. Wanna make me look good?

SARAH: Faster, huh?

5

JAMES: *(Thinking she's agreed to cooperate)* Okay. Thank you.

SARAH: Faster. Move it. Fly. Speed.

JAMES: I didn't understand that.

SARAH: *(In slow Signed English)* If you do not sign faster, the hour will be over before you finish your opening speech.

JAMES: Oh, if! If. I. Do. Not. Sign. Fast. Er. The hour will be over before I finish my opening speech.

(It takes him a moment to comprehend "If"—she's doing it very slowly. As she goes on, her signing becomes faster, ending in a blur, James' voice trailing behind)

JAMES: Are you doing this because I'm not deaf? I used to pretend to be deaf, if that counts. Look—you can't do this to me. I was in the Peace Corps for three years—I saved Ecuador

(It takes him a while to finger spell Ecuador)

—so I'm scheduled for a lot of success here, if you know what I mean.

(Nope)

Well—good—okay. Why don't you come back and see me sometime and we'll have the same fun again.

SARAH: You give up easier than most.

JAMES: I give up easier than most?

SARAH: That's smart.

JAMES: Smart. Thank you.

(She goes. After she's gone)

Right—you can go.

MRS. NORMAN: *(Entering)* If you don't mind, Mr. Leeds, I really don't feel like going through another interrogation about Sarah. I've come to feel like a mandatory stop in some training program for new teachers at the school.

6

JAMES: Mrs. Norman, your daughter's file indicates she hasn't been home here since she was eighteen.

MRS. NORMAN: That's correct.

JAMES: May I ask why?

MRS. NORMAN: We sent Sarah away to the school when she was five, Mr. Leeds. When she decided not to visit us anymore, she didn't consult me.

JAMES: But you went out there to visit her.

MRS. NORMAN: I tried. Then I stopped.

JAMES: I see.

MRS. NORMAN: Then you're unique among the teachers who've come calling here the past twenty-one years.

JAMES: Mrs. Norman, Sarah's twenty-six years old. The only reason they let her stay at the school at her age is because she works and goes through the motions of attending classes. Did you know she's a maid in the dorms?

MRS. NORMAN: No. I didn't. I'm sure you have an alternative in mind, though.

JAMES: Well, her test scores indicate exceptional intelligence.

MRS. NORMAN: Come on, now say: There's still time, there's still hope.

JAMES: There's still time, there's still hope.

MRS. NORMAN: For what?

JAMES: For her to achieve the communication skills to get into college or at least a good trade school.

MRS. NORMAN: Communication skills? In other words, you're still trying to force her to speak and lip read so she can pass for hearing.

JAMES: No, what I'm trying to *force* on her is the ability to function in the same world you and I do.

MRS. NORMAN: As if that were something to aspire to. Now, will that be all, Mr. Leeds?

JAMES: No—is Mr. Norman here? If you won't—

MRS. NORMAN: Mr. Norman went away shortly after we sent Sarah to the school. I haven't seen or heard from him in

7

over twenty years. Now, Mr. Leeds, I will show you to the door.

(Mrs. Norman exits as Sarah enters)

JAMES: *(To Sarah)* I didn't think you were going to come back.

(She holds out a note to him. He takes it)

"Dear Sarah, Please see me tomorrow, I'll have some new routines. James Leeds." I wonder who wrote that. Want to play stand-up, sit-down again?

(She smiles a small smile)

Careful—you're smiling.

(She frowns)

Sorry. Are you coming in or not?

(She comes in. He writes "Sarah" on the blackboard syllabically, with accent and vowel markings)

"Sar-ah."

(She stamps her foot to get his attention)

SARAH: You burn your draft card?
JAMES: I'm sorry, did I burn my what?
SARAH: Draft. Card.
JAMES: Army. Card. Oh—my draft card.
SARAH: I heard you were a radical in college.
JAMES: You heard I was a ... in college. I'm sorry, I didn't get ...

(He indicates "radical." She writes "RADICAL" on the blackboard opposite her name)

Ah—you heard I was a radical in college. No. I burned my Blue Cross card.

SARAH: Why?

JAMES: I was afraid to burn my draft card. And the Blue Cross card wasn't going to be that useful in the Peace Corps.

SARAH: I don't understand.

JAMES: That's a joke.

SARAH: I don't see the humor.

JAMES: You don't see the humor? Now that we're talking, we don't seem to be understanding each other any better.

SARAH: Why should we?

JAMES: Why should we? Because I have learned all these techniques that are supposed to work. I wasn't exactly a radical. I was sort of left of liberal and right of radical.

SARAH: Where's that?

JAMES: Where's that? I still got my hair cut short before going home for major holidays.

SARAH: Why?

JAMES: Why? Well, my father scared me. He was a colonel in the army.

SARAH: Did he fight in the war?

JAMES: Not only did he fight in the war—he had billing above the title: "The United States presents Col. Walter J. Leeds in *The Vietnam War.*"

(He makes war noises)

SARAH: Another joke?

JAMES: Another joke, right. You're a terrific audience.

SARAH: Your timing is terrible and your signing is boring.

JAMES: My timing is terrible and my signing is boring. If you could hear, you'd think I was a scream.

SARAH: Why scream?

JAMES: Not literally "scream." That's a hearing idiom.

9

SARAH: But I'm deaf.

JAMES: You're deaf. I'll try to remember that.

SARAH: But you'll keep forgetting.

JAMES: I'll keep forgetting. But you'll keep reminding me.

SARAH: But you'll still forget.

JAMES: I'll still forget. But you'll still remind me.

SARAH: No. I'll give up.

JAMES: Maybe you won't have to give up.

SARAH: Why?

JAMES: Maybe I'll remember.

SARAH: I doubt it.

JAMES: We'll see.

SARAH: Right. Orin won't be so impressed when he finds out you weren't a radical.

JAMES: Orin won't be so impressed when he finds out I wasn't a radical. I'm here to teach, not to please Orin. Speaking of which ...

(He heads for the blackboard)

Oh, yesterday I had a really lousy visit with your mother.

SARAH: *(A burst of ASL)* I'm a big girl now. Why do you still have to ask my mother for information?

JAMES: What's the matter? Wait a second. I'm sorry. I didn't mean to do whatever I ... Look, what ... what—

SARAH: What! What!

JAMES: That's my best sign. What! Look, could we stop this, please? Why don't we ...

SARAH: What?

JAMES: ... sneak over the wall and go into town to this little Italian restaurant I discovered last weekend.

SARAH: You're crazy.

JAMES: Just say yes or no.

SARAH: *(A beat)* Yes.

JAMES: Good. I think. All right, I'll meet you in one hour in the trees behind the duck pond. I'll whisper your name.

SARAH: You're not funny.

JAMES: I think you *do* think I'm funny but you're afraid if you laugh you'll lose something. You know what I'm talking about? Hearing person, 1; deaf person, 0.

(Lydia has entered several lines earlier and seen the last of this from behind a corner of the blackboard. She laughs)

Oh Christ. Are you Lydia?

(Lydia stares at him. Nods)

How do you do. I'm Mr. Leeds, Lydia.

(He shows her his sign—an "L" to his heart. Sarah and Lydia laugh)

Hey, I'm getting some laughs here finally. Why are you laughing?

SARAH: You signed "lazy."

JAMES: I signed "lazy." *(Comparing the two signs)* Mr. Lazy—right. Another great start.

SARAH: If you can't handle her alone, whisper my name.

JAMES: If I can't handle her alone, whisper your name. You're very funny.

SARAH: I'm funnier than you and I would be a better teacher.

JAMES: You're funnier than I am and you'd make a better teacher. If you want to be a teacher, let me help you learn to speak and lip read.

SARAH: Screw you.

(She goes, looking back)

LYDIA: Bye, Sarah.

JAMES: Excuse me, I know that sign! That's one of the first things I learned—how to talk dirty.

11

(A beat. To Lydia)

Are you afraid of me?

LYDIA: No. Sarah.

JAMES: We're in the same boat.

LYDIA: In a boat?

JAMES: No, we're the same. She scares me too.

LYDIA: But you're the teacher.

JAMES: Teachers can't be scared?

LYDIA: Oh no. They have to teach.

JAMES: This one also has a lot to learn.

LYDIA: I'll teach you.

JAMES: I'll bet you will. Why don't you sit down right over there. "Lydia."

(He writes her name on the blackboard syllabically, with the accent and vowel markings)

LYDIA: Can we have our lesson in the same boat?

JAMES: What same boat?

LYDIA: On the duck pond.

JAMES: *(Doesn't know quite what she's talking about but wings it)*

Yeah. Maybe one of our lessons. Now, this is how we'll warm up for each session. Slide a little closer.

(He brushes her hair from her cheeks, revealing two large hearing aids running from her ears into her shirt pockets; obviously she uses her hair to try to camouflage the amplifiers)

I want you to listen, and watch my mouth, and then repeat exactly what I say.

(Sarah enters, her hair and/or attire slightly altered. She comes into the "restaurant," signifies "two," sits, looks at a menu as James and Lydia continue)

Aaaayyyy.

LYDIA: Aaaayyy.

JAMES: Eeeeee.

LYDIA: Eeeeee.

JAMES: Eeeeyyyyeee.

LYDIA: Eeeeyyyyeee.

JAMES: Oooohhhhh.

LYDIA: Oooohhhhh.

JAMES: Yooouuuuuu.

LYDIA: Yooouuuuuu.

JAMES AND LYDIA: *(Together)* Aaaayyyy.

JAMES: *(Joining Sarah)* What   LYDIA: *(Continuing by herself)*
would you like?   Eee, Eeyyee, Oohhh,
                                                    Yoouu.

(Lydia leaves)

(Sarah deliberates a moment, then points at something)

Dessert? You're sure you want to start with dessert?

(Embarrassed, she quickly tries to decipher the menu again)

Okay—wait—sure, I like the idea. We'll both start with
dessert.

SARAH: Wait.

(A beat)

Help me.

JAMES: I'd be pleased to help you. Should I suggest something?

SARAH: Yes.

JAMES: *(Not signing, to himself)* Well, the veal piccata is nice.

(James mouthing, as for a lip reader)

13

Veal piccata.

(Sarah looks away, rejecting that form of communication, forcing James to finger spell)

I'm sorry. V-e-a-l [p-i-c-c-a-t-a.] See, by the time I finish spelling it, they may be out of it.

SARAH: What is it?

JAMES: That's veal sauteed in lemon and butter.

SARAH: What's veal?

JAMES: What's veal? Well—what the hell is veal? How do you sign calf? -a-l-f.

SARAH: Cow baby.

JAMES: Cow baby. Makes sense. Would you like some of that?

SARAH: No.

JAMES: No, I suppose cow baby sauteed in lemon and butter doesn't really sound ...

SARAH: What I really want is pasta.

JAMES: What you really want is p-a—pasta. Now we're talking.

SARAH: ... with cheese ...

JAMES: With cheese.

SARAH: ... garlic ...

JAMES: And garlic.

SARAH: ... herbs ...

JAMES: Herbs.

SARAH: ... meat. Stuffed inside.

JAMES: And meat. Stuffed in—Ah! You've just described a dish it'll take me another hour to spell. C-a-n-n-e-l-l-o-n-i.

SARAH: Try.

JAMES: Okay. What to drink?

SARAH: Milkshake.

(The deaf sign for "milkshake" looks like the hearing symbol for "jerking off")

14

JAMES: What's that?

SARAH: Milkshake.

JAMES: Could you spell that please?

SARAH: *(Spelling)* M-i-l-k-s-h-a-k-e.

JAMES: M-i-l-k—That's the sign for milkshake?

SARAH: Yes.

JAMES: Ya know, in the hearing world ... Forget it.

(Silence. She's got it)

You don't want that with Italian food anyway. Help me, I'm dying!

SARAH: What do I want?

JAMES: You want wine. I mean, *do* you want wine?

SARAH: Can we?

JAMES: Of course we can. Should have wine with Italian food.

SARAH: Good.

JAMES: Okay. How 'bout a nap?

SARAH: Why are you trying to be different from the other hearing teachers?

JAMES: Why am I trying to be different from the other hearing teachers? Why did I have to bring you to an Italian restaurant to get you to talk to a hearing person?

SARAH: I don't need what you want to give me. I have a language that's just as good as yours!

JAMES: You don't need what I want to give you. Your language is just as good as mine—among the *deaf*, Sarah.

SARAH: Where's the garlic bread?

JAMES: Where's the garlic bread? Over there by the salad. Come on. I'll show you.

(They rise and move to the "salad bar." She seems confused)

You take a plate and help yourself.

(She does. He watches her)

Wouldn't you like to be able to function in the hearing world?

SARAH: No.

JAMES: No, I mean to be able to speak and lip read like Orin?

SARAH: Orin!

JAMES: Yeah.

(She draws a grotesque picture of Orin speaking—spitting, his mouth contorted)

Oh no, Orin doesn't look like that.

SARAH: Lydia!

JAMES: Lydia doesn't look like that either. People who are born deaf look like that sometimes.

SARAH: Always.

JAMES: Always? Oh yes, I know: Lesson number one in grad school: Very difficult to teach someone born deaf like you to speak and lip read, because you've never heard the sound of a human voice—okay? But it can be done. *(Sarah looks away. James gets her attention)* I mean it. What's more exciting than something truly difficult? Sure, it's easier for Orin and Lydia because they can hear a little bit. All right, look, you and I can start with lip reading, whudduya say?

(She closes him off, returns to the table. He follows)

You like being a maid?

SARAH: Yes.

JAMES: Why?

SARAH: I like working alone. In my silence.

JAMES: Oh, come on, there are other jobs where a person can work alone and in silence.

SARAH: Not with toilet bowl cleaner.

16

JAMES: Not with toilet bowl cleaner. You should have told me
that was the attraction. You clearly have the intelligence
to—

(She concentrates on her food, closing him out again)

Okay, I give up. What do you want to talk about?

SARAH: I want to eat so we won't have our hands.

JAMES: You want to eat so we won't have our hands. Well, I
may just bury my face in the plate and keep talking.

(A beat)

SARAH: Talk about you.

JAMES: Talk about me. Okay. What do you want to
know?

SARAH: You said before that you used to pretend to be deaf.

JAMES: I said before that I used to pretend to be deaf. So you
were paying attention.

SARAH: How did you do that?

JAMES: How did I do that? That's easy. I just ...

(He puts his hands over his ears)

SARAH: Why?

JAMES: Why? Forget it.

SARAH: Come on, come on.

JAMES: All right. My mother was Jewish; she married a Catho-
lic who turned out to be an atheist; didn't matter because
my mother turned out to be of a faith heretofore unknown
to man. She designated me her confessor, complete with
semi-immaculate birth and healing powers.

SARAH: How?

JAMES: How? Well, I used to ... Demon ... come out! You
know—hands over the ears ...

(He starts to put his hands over her ears. She pulls away. He demonstrates on himself—snapping his hands away from his ears)

... like this.

SARAH: Where's the deaf part?

JAMES: Where's the deaf part? The time finally came when I had to stop hearing her, so I ...

(He indicates shutting his mother out. A beat—he disturbed)

Did you ever pretend to hear?

SARAH: No ... Yes. I used to pretend ...

JAMES: No. Yeah? Come on, tell me.

SARAH: Dance?

JAMES: You wanna dance?

SARAH: I can hear the music.

JAMES: How do you hear the music?

SARAH: Vibrations.

JAMES: Vibrations?

SARAH: *(Deadpan)* Through my nose.

JAMES: Through your nose?

(Sarah breaks into a smile. They move toward the dance floor)

There's nobody else dancing.

(They dance—managing to come together physically. Perhaps out of fear, unease, whatever, she pulls back and talks to him while they continue to dance)

SARAH: Why did you become a speech therapist?

JAMES: Why did I get into speech therapy? I don't know. Let's dance.

SARAH: Dance and talk.

JAMES: Dance and talk. No, that's too hard.

18

(He pulls her to him. They dance. She pulls back)

SARAH: Tell me.

(They dance and talk after all)

JAMES: In the sixties it seemed important to do things that weren't simply self-serving.

SARAH: Isn't this self-serving?

JAMES: This is self-serving? I guess it is, in that it feels good to help people.

SARAH: But you're not helping anyone.

JAMES: I'm not helping anyone? That's your opinion.

SARAH: You're lucky.

JAMES: Why am I lucky?

SARAH: Because you believe in something you're doing, even though you're not doing it.

JAMES: Because I believe in something I'm doing, even though I'm not doing it.

(She looks at her watch. Time to go. She moves back to the table; he follows)

You know, you too could believe in something you're not doing.

SARAH: *(Mouthing)* Blah, blah, blah.

JAMES: Speech—right. Can I help you?

(He helps her with her sweater. They walk in silence "outdoors")

SARAH: So your mother told you you were God.

JAMES: So my mother told me I was God. Yes, that's correct.

SARAH: And that's why you want to make me over in your image.

JAMES: And that's why I want to make you over in my image. Okay.

19

SARAH: Only one problem.

JAMES: Only one problem—I thought there'd be at least two.

SARAH: I don't believe in God.

JAMES: You don't believe in ... Now, wait a minute. I thought deaf people were required to believe in God. Sure! The damned of God who must perform a lifetime of penance.

SARAH: *(Putting her hands to her ears)* Demon, come out! Why always over the ears?

JAMES: Demon come out! Yeah. Why always over the ears? I don't know.

(She puts her hand to his head, his belly)

SARAH AND JAMES: Why not over the head, over the belly ...

SARAH: ... over the mouth.

(A beat, her hand to his mouth; removed)

Time?

JAMES: Curfew.

SARAH: Bye.

JAMES: *(Stopping her)* I've really enjoyed this evening with you.

SARAH: Me too.

(Sarah thinks he'll kiss her but after a moment he offers his hand. They shake and part.

Orin, with an Ojo de Dios, a diamond shaped piece made of multi-colored yarn strung to a wooden frame)

JAMES: May I come in?

ORIN: Hello, Mr. Leeds.

JAMES: You missed our session, Orin. Are you sick?

ORIN: I am busy making these to sell on Parents' Day to a lot of guilty parents who will hide them in the closet. I'm not sick, Mr. Leeds, so if that's what you came to find out ...

20

JAMES: Wait a minute, is there something wrong? Between us?

(Orin focuses on his Ojo. James gets his attention)

> Orin, I need some advice on how to get Sarah Norman to speak.

ORIN: Is that what you want?

JAMES: Excuse me?

ORIN: Why did you go out to dinner with Sarah?

JAMES: How did you—

ORIN: Oh yes, we know: You want to help her.

JAMES: Yes, I—

ORIN: You don't fool us. You think learning to sign means you can communicate with us, that because you want to change us we want to be changed.

JAMES: Oh Orin, for Christ's—

ORIN: One of these days, Mr. Leeds, I'm going to change this system that sticks us with teachers who pretend to help but really want to glorify themselves!

JAMES: I do want to help, Orin, you have to believe that.

ORIN: No, Mr. Leeds, I don't have to. You have to. I thought you were different.

JAMES: Listen, don't lump me together with a bunch of incompetent—

ORIN: Now, if you don't mind, please leave my room.

JAMES: Orin, can't we sit down and talk this over?

ORIN: No thank you. And, oh, by the way, I have had veal piccata. Yes. And I have had other *"hearing"* food.

JAMES: "Hearing food"?

ORIN: Raw fish. Japanese. Zugee.

JAMES: No, sushi.

(Orin goes angrily)

> I'm sorry, Orin. I'm sorry ...

LYDIA: *(Entering)* Hello, Mr. Leeds.

JAMES: Oh, Lydia, I'm sorry I'm late.

LYDIA: I am reading your book.

JAMES: *(Blocking it as if it might attack him)* My old Child Psychology book!

LYDIA: Psy ...

JAMES: Psychology. There's a good word for you. Ssss ...

(He writes the "P" on the chalk board)

Sssssychology.

(He writes the rest of the word)

LYDIA: What does it mean?

JAMES: Cracking open people's heads. Why people do what they do.

LYDIA: Why do they?

JAMES: If I ever figure that one out, I'll let you know.

LYDIA: I'm having trouble with the first sentence.

JAMES: Ah, one of the greats. How could I forget. "Ontogeny recapitulates phylogeny." Psychology students all over the world have read those words and moved into other fields.

LYDIA: What does it mean?

JAMES: It means that ... that we make ourselves over in our own image.

LYDIA: Oh, good.

JAMES: Want to sit down?

(Lydia sits)

LYDIA: Mr. Leeds ... that other night, you ate by yourself, huh? In a restaurant in town. Boy, that's lonesome, huh, eating alone? I ate by myself in the cafeteria. I read two books. I read what you told me to practice.

JAMES: Oh really? Let me hear a little bit of it then.

22

LYDIA: *(Very carefully articulating)* Thank you, Tom Turkey, for thinking of Thanksgiving.

JAMES: Hey! Good for you. You did practice.

LYDIA: I know. Will you be eating in the cafeteria on Thanksgiving?

JAMES: Maybe I will.

LYDIA: I could eat with you. I won't read a book.

JAMES: We could just talk.

LYDIA: Okay! I'll read this for tomorrow.

(She takes the book and starts to leave. We hear a whistle)

JAMES: What was that noise?

LYDIA: My hearing aid. Whenever I smile, it whistles. See you soon.

(Lydia goes. We're at the "duck pond" after dinner. Sarah touches James, hands him a note)

JAMES: Well, at last. "Dear Sarah, Please meet me at the duck pond after dinner. I'll bring the stale bread. James Leeds."

(A beat)

How many people did you tell about our going over the wall?

SARAH: Not many.

JAMES: Not many. Orin was very upset.

SARAH: Orin thinks he's the guardian of all us deaf children because he's an apprentice teacher and speaks.

JAMES: Orin thinks he's the guardian of all you deaf children because he's an apprentice teacher and speaks.

SARAH: And he wants to lead a revolution against the hearing world and thinks we can hardly wait to follow him.

JAMES: And he wants to lead a revolution against the hearing world and he thinks you all can hardly wait to follow him.

23

When his revolution begins, he can have all my old Indian headbands and wire rim glasses.

SARAH: You think it's funny to want to do something for your people?

JAMES: Do I think it's funny to want to do something for my people?

SARAH: How would you like to spend your life in an institution, in a world run by people who don't understand you?

JAMES: How would I like to spend my life in an institution, in a world run by people who don't understand me? Why don't you go on the warpath with Orin?

SARAH: This isn't stale bread.

JAMES: Right, the bread is not stale. I feel good so I thought I'd bring some fresh bread.

SARAH: Why do you feel good?

JAMES: Because I missed you.

SARAH: Don't say that.

JAMES: I haven't seen you for days. You've been avoiding me. I even ate lunch in the cafeteria, thinking I'd see you.

SARAH: I've been eating in the kitchen so you wouldn't see me.

JAMES: You've been eating in the kitchen so I wouldn't see you. Well, I didn't see you. You know, I hate to say this, but you're the most mysterious, attractive, angry person I've ever met.

SARAH: Why did you miss me?

JAMES: Why did I miss you? Why do people miss each other?

(Sarah becomes conscious of Lydia who has moved in to feed the ducks too)

SARAH: Go! Get out of here!

JAMES: *(Calling after her)* Wait! Oh that's all right, Lydia! Wait a ... Come back ...

(She's gone)

That was a bit rough, wasn't it?

SARAH: Should I treat her like she's handicapped?

JAMES: You think the only alternative to treating someone like they're handicapped is to treat them like that?

SARAH: Yes!

JAMES: You should get out of the toilet cleaning business and give some seminars on interpersonal relationships.

SARAH: She's going to become dependent on you.

JAMES: Would that be so terrible if she became dependent on me?

SARAH: She'll fall in love with you.

JAMES: She's gonna fall in love with me. You know, all students don't automatically—Jesus Christ, that's quite a little leap you made there; from helping someone to learn something to dependency because of it, to falling in love as a result of the dependency. That's very nice, but it happens to be bullshit. You have a sign for b-u-l-l shit?

SARAH: Bullshit. *(A bull's horns with one hand; at the other end, a closed fist with the other hand; the closed fist springs open in James' face)* You're trying to con everyone.

JAMES: Excuse me, I'm trying to what everybody?

SARAH: C-o-n everybody.

JAMES: C-o-n. No, not everybody—only you. Wait a second, I'm going to invent a little sign here. Deaf-bullshit. *(The same sign as above with one horn stuck in his ear)*

SARAH: I have to go.

JAMES: You have to go? Fine, take your deaf-bullshit and go.

(Sarah starts to leave but James blocks her way. She forces his arms to his side and holds them there, stopping the "deaf-bullshit" sign. He kisses her. She breaks free)

SARAH: You didn't con me.

JAMES: It's always worked before. See, when I get in trouble, I kiss the girl and make everything better.

(She goes)

Oh, come on, Sarah!

(He chases her)

Sarah ... !

FRANKLIN: *(Entering from opposite side)* Yelling at the back of a deaf person. That's very good, Mr. Leeds. Problems?

JAMES: No. Just trying out a new technique.

FRANKLIN: What's it called—rape? ... Mr. Leeds.

JAMES: Yes.

FRANKLIN What are you doing here with Sarah?

JAMES: Feeding the ducks.

FRANKLIN: Ah. Why?

JAMES: Because they're hungry.   FRANKLIN: Because they're hungry.

FRANKLIN: Mr. Leeds—James—Jimbo, we don't fornicate with the students. We just screw them over. If you ever get the two confused ... you're gone.

(Franklin goes)

JAMES: I wasn't trying to screw her over, you damned ... I was just trying to—

MRS. NORMAN: *(Entering)* I usually don't get the second visit, Mr. Leeds.

JAMES: I promise if I don't strike gold this time, I'll give up like all the others.

MRS. NORMAN: I'm not sure you will. Give up, that is. There are people, I understand, who revel in failure.

JAMES: The guy who taught the Ecuadorians to grow and love brussels sprouts isn't gonna be scared off by the insults of a guilt-ridden mother.

MRS. NORMAN: I want you to leave my home.

JAMES: Look, Mrs. Norman, I know this is difficult—

MRS. NORMAN: You don't know what difficult is. Teaching speech to a retarded child deaf from birth is impossible. Give up!

JAMES: Wait a minute. Sarah is not retarded! They just thought she was until she was twelve.

MRS. NORMAN: First they said she was, then they said she wasn't! What are they saying now?

JAMES: That she's only deaf.

MRS. NORMAN: Only deaf.

JAMES: She is not retarded! She's capable of learning anything.

MRS. NORMAN: Then *you* teach her.

JAMES: That's what I'm trying to do! Help me. Please. Tell me, did Sarah ever try to speak?

MRS. NORMAN: She stopped trying when it became important to her how she looked to my friends and most of all to her sister's friends.

JAMES: How she looked?

MRS. NORMAN: Yes. She looked grotesque. She was afraid people would still think she was retarded.

JAMES: Like you did.

MRS. NORMAN: I don't know what I thought! I have stopped thinking about what I thought!

JAMES: I'm sorry. When Sarah came home on weekends, did she and her sister's friends go out together? What did they do? ... Come on, Mrs. Norman, please.

(A beat)

MRS. NORMAN: There came a time when I could no longer tolerate the two of us in this house trying frantically to discover things we might do together—read, cook, sew—Here, look, see, we're having a nice, normal visit. So I asked—no, I demanded that her sister Ruth ask her boyfriend's friends to become companions for Sarah and

27

we would owe them dearly in another life. Well, it worked.
I mean, you should have seen her. These boys really liked
Sarah, treated her the same way they treated Ruth, with
respect and ... and if you didn't know there was a problem,
you'd have thought she was a perfectly normal ...

(A beat)

Well, you just can't understand.

(A beat)

You're making me pity myself now, Mr. Leeds. It's been a
long time. I would appreciate it if you wouldn't come back
a third time. Please.

(She goes)

JAMES: *(To Sarah, who is pushing a maid's cleaning cart. She
begins cleaning the blackboard with a wet rag)*

Hello. I left you a note. It said: "Please see me this afternoon, I'll bring the boxing gloves." You didn't come so I
ate all the gloves myself. I'm sorry to interrupt your work.

SARAH: What do you want now?

JAMES: What do I want now? Okay, I want to know if you
think you *can't* learn to speak, that you're not capable?

SARAH: *(Pushing the blackboard upstage out of the way)* Not
speech talk again.

JAMES: *(Helping her with the blackboard)* Yeah, speech talk
again. You're not retarded—you know that?

SARAH: Since I was twelve.

(She begins to sweep)

JAMES: Since you were twelve—right. But do you really believe
it?

SARAH: What are you talking about?

JAMES: What am I talking about? I want to know if your hatred of hearing people has as much to do with us as it does with your hatred of you.

SARAH: That sounds like it came straight from a textbook.

JAMES: Well it did come right out of a textbook, but I think it's true anyway. Did not going home anymore after you were eighteen—did that have anything to do with your sister's friends? The boys you were going out with?

(She's silent)

Let me help you, damn it!

SARAH: How—by showing me the joys of sex with a hearing man?

JAMES: How—by showing you the joys of sex with a hearing man? You mean you and me? I don't see you making yourself available for that kind of therapy. I think that's one language you don't speak.

SARAH: You don't know what you're talking about!

JAMES: All right, you tell it to me right so I *will* know what I'm talking about!

SARAH: You're so ...

JAMES: I'm so what? What am I? Nosy? Stupid? Misguided? Come on—whatever it is, I can take it.

(She lets him have it)

SARAH: I have more than enough communication skills. You don't. They never did.

JAMES: I have more than enough communication skills. You don't. They never did. They? Who's they?

SARAH AND JAMES: *(James translates now in the first person)*
Hearing boys. They could never be bothered learning my language. No—that was too difficult. I was always expected to learn to speak. Well, I don't speak! I don't do things I can't do well. The boys who did try to communicate with me got about as far as: How are you, I am fine.

(A beat)

At first I let them have me because they would. Sex was something I could do as well as hearing girls. Better! It got to be that when I went home, the boys would be lined up on a waiting list my sister kept for me. Most of them didn't even take me for a Coke first. No introductions. No conversations. We just went straight to a dark place and [screwed]. But I liked that communication. I loved it. It made me feel a lot better than this bullshit talk you make.

(She finishes her sweep up)

SARAH: Now, does that explain everything?

JAMES: No, it doesn't explain everything, but it explains a little.

SARAH: That's all you're going to find out.

(She begins to rub furniture polish into a bench)

JAMES: No, that's not all I'm going to find out.

SARAH: I live in a place you can't enter. It's out of reach.

JAMES: You live in a place I can't enter. Out of reach? That sounds romantic.

SARAH: Deafness isn't the opposite of hearing, as you think. It's a silence full of sound.

JAMES: Deafness isn't the opposite of hearing, as I think. It's a silence full of sound. Really? A silence full of sound?

SARAH: The sound of spring breaking up through the death of winter.

(He doesn't understand the juxtaposition of: "winter" ... "earth" ... "broken" ... "growth" which is how she begins the line; yet, he is moved by it)

JAMES: The sound of ... What does that mean?

(Suddenly there is a softness, a closeness between them)

30

SARAH: My secret. No hearing person has ever gotten in here to find out ... No person, period.

JAMES: Your secret. No hearing person has ever gotten in there to find out ... No person, period.

(She runs from him. A beat. Night. He "climbs" a "tree." He tries to get Sarah's attention at her "window" as she reenters)

Hey! Open the window!

(She spots him in the "tree," but doesn't open the "window." He hangs onto the tree)

Usually, I kiss the girl and make everything better, remember? You didn't like that one, so I climbed this tree. Tough to resist a guy who climbs trees for you, isn't it?

SARAH: What if you get caught?

JAMES: What if I get caught? The hero —

(He almost falls)

Aauugh!

(He clutches the "tree")

The hero never gets caught on an important mission. Oh, I have another note for you. It says: "By the way, I'm terrified of heights. James Leeds." Please let me in.

(She throws the "window" open. He jumps into the room. Shy with each other but wanting to touch)

I don't want to be like those other guys. I want to take you for a Coke first. And I want to learn to communicate with you in whatever language we both can learn to speak. I like you. I really like you.

SARAH: Why? I'm terrible to you.

JAMES: Why? You're terrible to me? No, you're delightful to me—affectionate and sympathetic to a fault.

31

(A beat)

SARAH: I thought you'd give up in the beginning.

SARAH: Why? I'm terrible to you.

JAMES: Why? You're terrible to me? No, you're delightful to me—affectionate and sympathetic to a fault.

(A beat)

SARAH: I thought you'd give up in the beginning.

JAMES: You thought I'd give up in the beginning. Nope.

SARAH: I knew after what I told you yesterday, I wouldn't see you again.

JAMES: You knew after what you told me yesterday, you'd never see me again.

(He indicates: Here I am)

SARAH: You're the nicest person I've ever known.

JAMES: I'm the nicest person you've ever known. Do you mean that?

SARAH: But you scare me.

JAMES: But I scare you? I don't mean to.

SARAH: I don't think I trust you.

JAMES: You don't think you trust me? Take a chance.

SARAH: I can't. You better go.

JAMES: *(A beat; disappointed)* Okay ... Goodnight.

(He dives for window. She stops him. They embrace and move to the "bed." He starts to "turn the light out")

SARAH: Leave the light on.

JAMES: Leave the light on?

SARAH: So we can talk.

JAMES: So we can talk? During or afterward?

32

SARAH: Hard to talk during.

JAMES: Hard to talk during.

SARAH: Need my hands.

JAMES: You need your hands. I need my mouth.

SARAH: Silence.

(They come together)

ORIN: *(Entering)* I know what is going on between you and
         Sarah. For weeks now half the girls' dormitory has seen
         you climbing in and out of her window. Of course, you
         might have been going in there to coach her in speech.

LYDIA: *(Entering opposite)* Mr. Leeds, hi.

JAMES: Shhh!

LYDIA: What are you doing in my tree?

JAMES: I'm not in your tree, Lydia.

LYDIA: You're not looking for Sarah.

JAMES: Sarah who? For Chrissake, shut your damn window!

LYDIA: *(To Sarah)* He's eating at my table on Thanksgiving,
         you know!

(Lydia and Sarah slam their windows at each other. Lydia goes)

ORIN: It would not be hard for Mr. Franklin to find out what's
         going on.

JAMES: Look, Orin, if you're in love with Sarah, I'm sorry.

ORIN: I am not in love with anyone, Mr. Leeds.

JAMES: That's something to be proud of.

ORIN: But I need her and you don't.

JAMES: She's not going to stop being your friend just because—

ORIN: I need her for what we're going to do for deaf people.

JAMES: What you and *Sarah* are going to do?

ORIN: Believe me, I'm not some joker who burns his Blue
         Cross Card!

(Orin goes as Franklin crosses upstage)

FRANKLIN: Sit down, please, Mr. Leeds.

JAMES: *(Freezing in the "tree")* Orin ... !

FRANKLIN: Mr. Leeds, I've heard a rumor I'd like to share with you to give you an idea of the flights of fancy that deaf people are capable of.

JAMES: *(To Sarah)* Franklin knows.

SARAH: How?

JAMES: I don't know how. Someone must have told him.

SARAH: Who?

JAMES: Orin maybe ... ?

SARAH: No.

(Franklin crosses over again. James and Sarah take cover)

FRANKLIN: I'm told that if I were to station myself in the elm trees outside the girls' dormitory just after curfew ...

JAMES: I can't come here anymore. Franklin would fire me he found out.

SARAH: Who would have told him?

JAMES: Any number of people could have told him.

LYDIA: *(Entering; speaking and not signing, in effect closing Sarah out)* Hi, guys. What's new?

JAMES: How are you, Lydia?

LYDIA: Oh, I'm fine.

JAMES: Good, good.

SARAH: Is it time for her lesson?

JAMES: No, she doesn't have a lesson with me today.

SARAH: Did you tell Franklin something about Mr. Leeds and me?

JAMES: Yeah.

34

LYDIA: I have to go to handicrafts now, Mr. Leeds. I'll see you tomorrow.

JAMES: Just a minute, answer Sarah's question. Did you tell Franklin anything—

LYDIA: I'll see you tomorrow.

(Lydia runs off)

SARAH: I told you she'd fall in love with you.

JAMES: Oh, she's not in love with me.

SARAH: Maybe you should climb in her window one night.

JAMES: Maybe I should climb in her window some night? You're jealous.

SARAH: *(Illustrating)* She's dumb. Big breasts. Just what men want. Fondle her butt. Fondle her breasts.

JAMES: Is that really what men want? I'll tell you something, I happen to despise large breasts. You couldn't even give me a pair; if you had large breasts I wouldn't be sitting here having this ridiculous—

SARAH: Pimples!

JAMES: Those are not pimples. Those are perfectly charming, more than adequate ... Jesus Christ, you're a human being.

(As Franklin crosses this time, James slips innocently into step with him, as if they were strolling along having a conversation)

FRANKLIN: Lemme tell you something that I might seem out of place disclosing to you. You remember the day I brought Sarah to you I told you she'd worked so hard for the speech guy here before you ...

(Franklin leaves. Sarah looking out her "window." James slipping up behind Sarah carrying a gift behind his back; he startles her)

JAMES: Sorry I'm late. I got held up.

SARAH: Robbed?

JAMES: No, not robbed. Held up. Delayed.

SARAH: How did you get in?

JAMES: How did I get in? Through the cellar window, up the back steps, and down the hall on tip-toe.

SARAH: You're crazy.

JAMES: I had to see you.

(They kiss. He hands her the gift box. She opens it. A shawl)

I knitted it in handicrafts.

(She puts on the shawl, is delighted with it. A beat)

Can I ask you something?

SARAH: Yes.

JAMES: Franklin was kind enough to tell me you had a relationship with the speech therapist before me.

SARAH: *(A beat)* True.

JAMES: Franklin fired him when he found out ... ?

SARAH: Yes.

JAMES: Was he a hearing person?

SARAH: No, hard of hearing.

JAMES: Hard of hearing. You didn't want to leave with him?

SARAH: He didn't ask me.

JAMES: He didn't ask you.

SARAH: Hard of hearing people think they're better than deaf people.

JAMES: Hard of hearing people think they're better than deaf people. Do you still carry a torch for him?

SARAH: *(She doesn't get James' sign for "torch")* What?

JAMES: I made that up. Do you still ... hurt?

SARAH: No, I never hurt from other people.

JAMES: No? You never hurt from other people. What if you admitted that you do hurt?

36

SARAH: *(A beat)*

I would shrivel up and blow away.

JAMES: You would shrivel up and blow away.

(A beat)

Sarah, what if you and I left here together?

SARAH: What?

JAMES: What if you and I went to live in the city somewhere?

SARAH: I couldn't.

JAMES: Why couldn't you? You're scared? You'd get unscared.

SARAH: What would I do?

JAMES: You could do whatever you want to do. What do you want to do?

SARAH: I want to teach in a deaf school.

JAMES: You want to teach in a deaf school. That's possible. What else do you want?

SARAH: I want you.

JAMES: You've got me. What else do you want?

SARAH: House.

JAMES: A house—uh-oh.

SARAH: And car. Plant a garden and ...

JAMES: A car. Yeah, plant a garden ...

SARAH: So much! *(Drawing a picture with her hands)* Microwave oven!

JAMES: So much. *(Guessing Sarah's sign after a moment of puzzlement)* A microwave oven! How about a blender?

SARAH: Yes.

JAMES: *(Inventing a new sign)* How about a food processor!

SARAH: What?

JAMES: That's a blender that's smarter than a blender.

SARAH: I want one!

JAMES: You'll have two of them! What else? Come on. Too late to stop now.

37

SARAH: Children.

JAMES: Children.

SARAH: Deaf children.

JAMES: Deaf children.

(A beat)

What do you want me to say—that I want deaf children? I don't. But if they were, that would be all right.

SARAH: My father left us because I'm deaf.

JAMES: Your father left you because you were deaf. I am not going to do what your father did.

SARAH: What would you do if I went on with my schooling? Got a teaching certificate?

JAMES: What would I do if you went on with your schooling, got your teaching certificate? You mean here?

SARAH: Yes.

JAMES: I could still teach here, I guess, or I could finish my doctorate—What am I saying? We don't have to decide everything tonight.

SARAH: I want to.

JAMES: I know you want to, but we can't. The point is, it's all possible. And you know it. Say it. Say: I know it's possible.

(A beat)

SARAH: I know it's possible.

ORIN: *(Entering)* It won't work! It can't work!

LYDIA: *(Entering opposite side)* Mr. Leeds, you're leaving.

JAMES: We haven't decided yet, Lydia.

ORIN: *(To Sarah)* So you can attract a hearing man. Is that so much?

LYDIA: I want to come live with you.

JAMES: What?

ORIN: Stay here and help me.

38

LYDIA: You have to keep teaching me.

ORIN: Do something for someone besides yourself for a change!

LYDIA: I could sleep on your floor in a sleeping bag.

SARAH: *(Indicating Lydia)* What?

JAMES: Lydia wants to come live with us.

SARAH: *(To Lydia)* No!

JAMES: Oh, Sarah.

(Lydia runs off)

ORIN: Hey, I want to tell you something.

JAMES: Oh, Lydia, come back.

ORIN: You have no right to turn her away from us.

JAMES: I have no intention—

ORIN: You go with him and you'll still be a maid. His maid!

JAMES: *(Yelling after Orin as he goes)*
    Hey!

(Franklin with a clipboard in his hand, on which his attention is focused)

FRANKLIN: So, will you be resigning at the end of the year?

JAMES: Resigning?

FRANKLIN: Not that I want you to leave. The bridge game needs you. And frankly, you're a promising teacher. But whether you intend it or not, you're about to uproot Sarah from the only home she's ever known.

JAMES: We're just moving across the street to faculty housing.

FRANKLIN: Not to be terribly metaphoric, Mr. Leeds, but that's a long distance. You're asking Sarah to step away from the community of the deaf.

SARAH: What's he saying?

JAMES: He's not saying anything important.

SARAH: You can't decide what I hear and don't hear.

39

FRANKLIN: She's right, Mr. Leeds. You can't decide what she hears and doesn't hear.

SARAH: You can't edit the conversation.

JAMES: I was not editing the conversation.

FRANKLIN: Pardon me, Mr. Leeds, it would seem you didn't like the implications I was making, so you chose not to tell Sarah.

SARAH: Now what?

JAMES: *(To Sarah)* He should be signing. *(To Franklin)* Mr. Franklin, would you mind—

FRANKLIN: Why don't you sign my part of the conversation for me.

JAMES: Why don't you sign your own conversation?

FRANKLIN: I've got to finish what I'm doing here, and it'll give you a little practice.

JAMES: Practice at what?

SARAH: What is he saying?

FRANKLIN: *(Not signing, forcing James to sign it)* I'm saying I think James should get a taste of being a translator as that's one of the problems facing him each and every time the two of you venture into the hearing world.

(Franklin keeps his head to his clipboard)

SARAH: One of our problems! And what are the rest? Aren't you going to tell us the rest?

FRANKLIN: I'm sorry, Jimbo, what did she say?

JAMES: Oh, for Chri—She wants to know if you aren't going to forewarn us of the rest of our problems as well.

FRANKLIN: *(Forcing James to continue translating)* I suspect neither of you wants to hear that. Well, I'm sure you've both given this a great deal of thought. I've got to run. Thank you for telling me about your plans. I hope you'll invite me to the wedding.

(By the time James finishes interpreting, Franklin is long gone. James very frustrated)

40

SARAH: He's right—you will be a translator.

JAMES: He's right? Oh, that I'll be a translator. The trick is to do a better job than I just did.

SARAH: Don't hate me for not learning to speak.

JAMES: Hate you for not learning to speak? No, I'll love you for having the strength to be yourself.

(Mrs. Norman enters. She hasn't seen her daughter in eight years. She struggles to communicate with Sarah, more through gesture than sign)

MRS. NORMAN: Congratulations, Sarah. I'm very happy to see you. You're so grownup. You're ... Eight years. My, a person can't digest that in ...

(Sarah does not understand Mrs. Norman's sign)

I don't know how to say that.

(A beat. To James)

She didn't want to come, did she? You made her.

JAMES: You don't *make* Sarah do anything, Mrs. Norman.

SARAH: Tell me.

MRS. NORMAN: *(Managing to communicate, if haltingly)* I said, you didn't want to come. I don't know why you've come.

SARAH: I don't either. To hurt you maybe.

MRS. NORMAN: *(To James)* I'm sorry, I'm rusty—what did she say?

(Sarah insists on her mother's attention)

SARAH: *(Very slowly)* To h-u-r-t you. Maybe.	MRS. NORMAN: H. U. R. To hurt me. Maybe.

SARAH: To show you I've done fine without you.

JAMES: To show you she's done fine without you.

(Silence: mother and daughter. Then Sarah breaks, begins to look around the "house")

MRS. NORMAN: Do your parents know?

JAMES: No, my mother's dead and my father and I haven't spoken for several years.

SARAH: Can we spend the night in my old room?

JAMES: Sarah would like to know if we can spend the night in her old room.

(A beat)

MRS. NORMAN: If she'll promise to make conversation with me at breakfast in the morning.

JAMES: [If you promise to make conversation with her at breakfast in the morning.]

(A beat)

SARAH: Try.

JAMES: She'll try.

MRS. NORMAN: Yes, I remember that sign. [Try.]

(Mrs. Norman recedes as the scene shifts)

SARAH: My room.

JAMES: Your old room? Bit spare.

SARAH: I threw everything out the last time I came.

JAMES: You threw everything out the last time you came. You can't destroy that time by throwing things away.

SARAH: I did.

(James picks her up and carries her into the room)

JAMES: Small bed.

SARAH: That's why I want to sleep in it with you.

JAMES: That's why you want to spend the night in it with me.

SARAH: No man has been in this room since I was five. That was the night before they sent me to school.

JAMES: No man has been in this room since you were five. That was the night before they sent you away to the school.

SARAH: My father stayed with me that night. He cried. I never saw him again.

JAMES: Your father stayed with you that night. He cried. You never saw him again.

SARAH: After he left, my mother put a picture of the Virgin Mary on the wall; one weekend when I came to visit, I drew a hearing aid in her ear. My mother cried.

JAMES: After he left, your mother put a picture of the Virgin Mary on the wall; one weekend when you came to visit, you drew a hearing aid in her ear. Your mother cried. Yes, I can imagine.

SARAH: The next visit there was a picture of Ricky Nelson.

JAMES: The next visit there was a picture of Ricky Nelson. Makes sense. Why Ricky Nelson?

SARAH: I don't know. I never asked, she never explained.

JAMES: You never asked, she never explained.

SARAH: Nothing else on my walls.

JAMES: Nothing else on the walls.

SARAH: Just that picture: "To Sarah, Good Luck, From Ricky." In my mother's handwriting.

JAMES: Just that picture: "To Sarah, Good Luck, From Ricky." In your mother's handwriting.

(A beat)

Your mother wanted very much to touch you tonight. But you ... Maybe you wanted to touch her.

SARAH: I can't give more than I gave.

JAMES: You can't give more than you gave? I wonder. Maybe you could. You hardly ever get a second chance to ...

(James turns away)

SARAH: What are you talking about?

JAMES: Nothing. Forget it. None of my business.

SARAH: Tell me.

JAMES: Just the way your mother was standing there, staring into space.

SARAH: You're hiding.

JAMES: I'm hiding? No, I'm not ... Yes, I am. You remember I told you my mother died two years ago ...

SARAH: Yes.

JAMES: She killed herself. My father had left her after twenty-eight years. Just strolled away. Left me to take care of her. She lived with me for almost three years. When I raised the rent, she ...

(A beat)

Look, I really don't think we're gonna fit on that little bed, whudduya say?

SARAH: Tell me the rest.

JAMES: Tell you what rest?

(She lifts his hands up, encouraging him to go on)

JAMES: All right. One night, instead of sitting on her bed pretending to listen to that day's outpouring of grievances against the world, I tried a little variation on the ritual. Nothing much, I just said to her, "I can't take care of you any more. The thought of living with you one more day makes me want to put a gun to one of our heads." She was very good. She picked a cracker crumb off her blanket. Helpfully, I took it from her, put it in my mouth. And she just sat there staring into space, until finally she smiled—not at me, but at some absent third party—and she said, "James can't save me; he never could. Amen." And then she turned out the light. I swallowed the cracker; she swallowed [the pills]. Her note said, "Don't blame

44

yourself. When I see you in heaven, I'll still give you a great big Jesus hug.''

(She takes him to her. He breaks)

I'm fine. I'm sorry.

SARAH: We're not so different. We were both born to parents who would have been better off without us.

JAMES: We're not so different, huh? We were both born to parents who would have been better off without us.

SARAH: I love you.

JAMES: Oh, Sarah, I love you too.

(They cling to each other. He breaks gently, moves downstage)

And the next day we were married by a Justice of the Peace, with Sarah's mother in attendance. The Justice didn't sign, of course, so I translated the ceremony for Sarah. When it was done, she said to me:

SARAH: Let no one, living or dead, absent or present, ever come between us.

JAMES: Let no one, living or dead, absent or present, ever come between us.

JAMES: And I promised.

SARAH: You and me. Joined.

(James turns toward Sarah. He begins to move toward her as the lights fade to black)

ACT TWO

James watches Sarah intently. Isolated in her silence, she is "making up" her face.

JAMES: Sarah Norman Leeds. My wife. Sarah Norman Leeds is deaf.

(He puts on a pair of airplane mechanic's sound mufflers, an effort to simulate deafness somehow. He slaps them, indicating he can't hear)

She suffers a sensory-neutral deficit of unknown etiology. The osseous structures in her head conduct no sound. She has no residual hearing, derives no benefit from amplification. This profound impairment may have resulted from pre-natal rubella or from the recessive trait in her family. Sarah Norman Leeds' deafness is not correctable by surgery. It is incurable.

(Mrs. Norman and Franklin enter from opposite sides and come together)

SARAH: Look at me—I'm like a nervous little kid. Why should I be nervous? Are *they* nervous? No! They're going to come in and look at me like a laboratory specimen—*My quiche!* Watch —I'll ruin it and they won't be able to rave that the deafie cooked a quiche.

MRS. NORMAN: If someone had told me a year ago I'd be playing bridge with you and my daughter, I wouldn't have believed it.

FRANKLIN: I explained to her she was destroying my bridge game, that she had to let him out once a week to play a couple of rubbers. To my astonishment, she informed me James was teaching her to play, and that we would soon meet in mortal combat.

FRANKLIN: Do you play standard Goren? Schencken?

MRS. NORMAN: Heavens, I haven't played bridge in so long, there's no telling what I'll play.

FRANKLIN: Great.

SARAH: *(To James)* If I make mistakes, don't get mad at me.

JAMES: I promise. If you make mistakes, I'll just smile.

FRANKLIN: *(Looking at his watch)* Eight-oh-two!

JAMES: *(To Sarah)* Ready to march into battle?

FRANKLIN: *(To Mrs. Norman)* We should have started by now.

SARAH: *(To James)* You can't embarrass me in front of them.

JAMES: I would never embarrass you in front of them—*What? You're bidding that! Oh no!*

FRANKLIN: We're leaving.

(James and Sarah move toward the "game")

(To Mrs. Norman) I've gotta have the north seat. You sit south. It's just a little superstition of mine. *(To James)* I thought maybe we scared you off.

47

MRS. NORMAN: *(Signing only to Sarah)* [Franklin's mean.]

JAMES: You're a bit early.

FRANKLIN: I'm not early, I'm right on the stroke of the hour.

JAMES: You're the boss.

(Mrs. Norman deals the "cards")

FRANKLIN: Now, no cheating, Sarah.

SARAH: Cheating?

FRANKLIN: I've seen deaf people who cheat like bandits at bridge.

MRS. NORMAN: One club.

JAMES: One diamond.

FRANKLIN: A seeming scratch of the nose—like this—six of a suit ... *(He scratches his nose with a "six," changes to a "seven")* ... seven. I'm sorry, what did you say, partner?

MRS. NORMAN: One club to James' one diamond.

FRANKLIN: I'll pass. A little tug of the shirt here like this ... *(Over the heart)* ... five hearts.

SARAH: I promise I won't cheat.

MRS. NORMAN: She promises she won't cheat.

FRANKLIN: Thank you, I sign fluently.

MRS. NORMAN: Of course, I'm sorry.

SARAH: Two spades.

FRANKLIN: Two spades?

SARAH: Right.

FRANKLIN: Fine, fine.

MRS. NORMAN: Three clubs.

FRANKLIN: Three clubs?

JAMES: I double.

MRS. NORMAN: Three clubs.

FRANKLIN: Three clubs?

JAMES: I double.

48

FRANKLIN: Uh-huh, uh-huh. Three clubs, huh?

MRS. NORMAN: Well, I thought—

FRANKLIN: *Pass.*

SARAH: Four hearts.

FRANKLIN: Four hearts?

MRS. NORMAN: Pass.

JAMES: Four spades.

FRANKLIN: Pass.

SARAH: Six spades.

FRANKLIN: Six spades!

SARAH: Right.

FRANKLIN: Fine. Terrific.

MRS. NORMAN: Pass.

(Silence. James studies his hand, looks at Sarah)

FRANKLIN: Ah, ah—no eye contact, please.

JAMES: Pass.

FRANKLIN: You'll forgive me for thinking that someone playing bridge for the first time isn't going to make a small
slam, so—no offense—but I double.

SARAH: Redouble.

JAMES: Wait a minute. You're redoubling? Do you know how
many points you're playing for?

SARAH: A lot.

JAMES: A lot—right. I'm the dummy.

MRS. NORMAN: My lead.

*(They play one round of the hand. Sarah scoops up the "cards"
and then James scoops her up as if the entire hand has been
played)*

JAMES: Oh, my god, she made it! I don't believe it!

(Mrs. Norman and Franklin rise to leave)

MRS. NORMAN: I hope we can play again sometime, Mr. Franklin.

FRANKLIN: Uh-huh.

JAMES: You amaze me!

FRANKLIN: Getting her to marry you, Jimbo, is one thing ...

MRS. NORMAN: *(To Sarah)* I'm very proud of you.

FRANKLIN: ... but getting her to play bridge ...

MRS. NORMAN: Thank you for inviting me.

FRANKLIN: I'd say the only thing more remarkable would be to get her to do the one thing you were hired to do.

JAMES: Get her to speak. I will.

FRANKLIN: Get her to speak.

MRS. NORMAN: See you again soon?

SARAH: Please.

FRANKLIN: Keep in mind—whatever your progress, I'm retiring at sixty-five.

(Mrs. Norman and Franklin go)

JAMES: I can't believe you played that well!

SARAH: Neither could they.

JAMES: Neither could they?

SARAH: She cooks a quiche, she bids her hand correctly.

JAMES: She cooks a quiche, she bids her hand correctly.

SARAH: They looked at me like a laboratory specimen.

JAMES: They looked at you like a laboratory specimen? I don't know about your mother, but I think Franklin was just trying to look down your dress.

SARAH: He'll expect me to speak by the end of the week.

JAMES: He'll expect you to speak by the end of the week. Well? ... Naw, I told him dreams of a public speaking career were

50

over—that in a moment of erotic madness I had bitten your tongue out of your mouth.

SARAH: The quiche was runny on the bottom.

JAMES: The quiche was runny on the bottom? No, it was perfect—what are you talking about?

SARAH: Don't protect me.

JAMES: Don't protect you?—Okay, it was a litle runny on the bottom.

SARAH: Oh, no!—I knew it. Why?

JAMES: Did you heat the cream first?

SARAH: No.

JAMES: Try heating the cream first.

SARAH: Why didn't you tell me?

JAMES: I didn't tell you because you didn't ask me.

SARAH: Since when has that stopped you?

JAMES: Since when has that stopped me? Didn't you enjoy this evening?

SARAH: No.

JAMES: I'm sorry. I thought you did.

SARAH: *(A beat)* I did.

JAMES: You did.

SARAH: Yes.

JAMES: Are you afraid if you let everybody know you're enjoying life in the hearing world they'll revoke your angry deaf person's license?

SARAH: Not funny.

JAMES: Not funny. I'm sorry.

(James has begun to prepare for bed. Orin enters but is unseen by either Sarah or James)

ORIN: All your friends across the road at the School for the Deaf—you remember the School for the Deaf—they're

51

very impressed with you, Sarah. You have a full-time interpreter just like a United Nations diplomat.

SARAH: *(Disturbed by this evocation of Orin)* Let's go for a
walk.

JAMES: Go for a walk? Now?

SARAH: Want to?   ORIN: You drive a car ...

JAMES: It's midnight.

SARAH: I've always wanted | ORIN: ... you shop by your-
to go out after midnight | self in food stores, you
without worrying about | have a checking account.
curfew. | You're a regular Ameri-
| can housewife.

JAMES: You've always wanted to go out after midnight without
worrying about curfew.

(They go out into the "night")

ORIN: Would you care to know that I have made contact with a
lawyer who is interested in the injustices being perpetrated
here?

(Edna Klein—the lawyer)

KLEIN: Dear Mr. Dennis, I was moved by your recent letter.

ORIN: What injustices? Tell me how many deaf people teach in
this institution.

KLEIN: I would be pleased to drive up and meet with you and
your friend, Miss Norman.

ORIN: Don't tell me I had no right to use your name. I say I
did.

KLEIN: I'm not sure what legal recourse you might have ...

(She exits)

ORIN: Look at me! Don't turn your back on me, Sarah!

(He exits)

SARAH: I like this best—what we can do alone together.

JAMES: You like this best—what we can do alone together. We can't always be alone ... What's the matter? You're not unremittingly joyous about what you did tonight.

SARAH: Little bothered.

JAMES: A little bothered about what?

SARAH: I feel split down the middle, caught between two worlds.

JAMES: You feel ... what?

SARAH: Deaf world here, hearing world here.

JAMES: Caught between the deaf and hearing worlds.

SARAH: I hope I'm strong enough to juggle both.

JAMES: You hope you're strong enough to juggle both. If you're not, I am. We're a team. We're unbeatable. Right?

SARAH: Yes.

JAMES: You didn't sign that with sufficient conviction. Try it again.

SARAH: Yes!

JAMES: Too much. Take it down a little bit.

SARAH: Yes.

JAMES: That's about right.

(She's still not comfortable with it all)

I'm telling you, you're going to bridge the two worlds brilliantly. Repeat after me: Boy, am I bent on being a brilliant bridger. Boy ...

SARAH: *(Mouthing it; no sound, no sign)* Boy.

JAMES: Hey, what was that? That's good! All you need to do is push a little air behind that and you'll have a spoken word. Boy ...

SARAH: You bit my tongue off.

JAMES: I bit your tongue out. Oh, Sarah, you lip read so many

53

words. If you'd stop seeing this speaking thing as a test of wills ...

SARAH: It's not. I'm too old to learn to speak and lip read well.

JAMES: It's not. You're too old to learn to speak and lip read well enough for *whom*?

SARAH: Me.

JAMES: For you. Yes, I know you *think* that.

SARAH: I've told you before—I don't do things I can't do well.

JAMES: You've told me before—you don't do things you can't do well. I still say—

SARAH: Please. I don't want to talk about this any more tonight.

JAMES: You don't want to talk about that any more tonight. What do you wanna do?

SARAH: Go home and practice my quiche.

JAMES: Go home and practice your quiche. I have a better idea. Why don't we go home and practice being alone together. Practice a particular kind of teamwork, if you follow my drift.

SARAH: I could be convinced.

JAMES: You could be convinced. What would it take to convince you?

SARAH: Nothing.

JAMES: Nothing. I love a girl who plays hard to get.

(She runs "inside." James follows)

I was only kidding!

(The "scene" shifts into mind-space. They stare at each other from a distance)

You amaze me. But what I don't know enough ... I need to know what it's like in there.

(He makes the sign which Sarah used earlier to describe her silence) [Break-Growth.]

(Sarah covers her ears with her hands. James does the same) [No.]

(She puts the sound-mufflers on his head. No good. James takes them off. They embrace)

(James, unsigned, to himself)

    I need to be ingested by you. Need somehow to penetrate and twist and burrow ...

LYDIA: *(Entering)* Hi, guys. Guess who came with some important news? Mr. Franklin gave me Sarah's job.

JAMES: Yes, we heard that.

LYDIA: Now I'm the official maid.

JAMES: Congratulations.

LYDIA: You have any tips for me?

SARAH: Yes. After you clean the toilet bowl ...

LYDIA: After you clean the toilet bowl—yeah?

SARAH: Get out before you flush.

LYDIA: Get out before you flush. What does that mean? *(To James)* Can I watch your new TV?

JAMES: How do you know we have a new TV?

LYDIA: Everybody knows you gave Sarah a credit card to buy new TV's.

JAMES: Ask Sarah.

LYDIA: Why do I have to ask her?

JAMES: It's her TV.

LYDIA: It's *your* TV.

JAMES: That's not right, Lydia.

SARAH: *(To Lydia)* What are you saying?

LYDIA: It was private.

JAMES: Go on—ask her.

LYDIA: Can I watch your new TV?

55

SARAH: Watch in the TV lounge.

LYDIA: I don't like to watch in the TV lounge. You always have to keep changing the volume on your hearing aid. Everyone is always fighting about how loud the sound should be. Yesterday, I almost had a nervous breakdown. I did. Really. *(To James, when Sarah appears unmoved)* Mr. Leeds ...

JAMES: Oh, come on, Sarah, let her watch your TV. It's good for her—she picks up the pronunciation of words.

SARAH: Fine. Go. Watch TV.

LYDIA: Yay!

(Lydia goes to watch "TV" in their "bedroom." James a bit disapproving of or surprised by Sarah's behavior)

SARAH: I don't want her hanging around here.

JAMES: You don't want her hanging around here. It's not going to hurt Lydia if we make her feel welcome.

SARAH: It's not going to hurt me if I have my privacy. You married me, not her.

JAMES: It's not going to hurt you if you have your privacy. I married you, not her—

LYDIA: Mr. Leeds ...

JAMES: *(To Sarah)* Wait a second. *(To Lydia)* What?

LYDIA: ... can I have one of your beers from your refrigerator?

JAMES: Sure, how 'bout a beer?

LYDIA: Okay!

SARAH: Now what?

JAMES: Nothing, not important. Now, what were you saying—

SARAH: *(Mimicking James)* Nothing, not important.

(Sarah moves away angrily)

JAMES: Nothing, not important. I'm sorry, I didn't mean to cut you off ... he said loudly into the silence.

(Silence is broken by loud TV sounds)

LYDIA: What did you say?

JAMES: I said turn the volume on that damn thing down!

LYDIA: What?

JAMES: Turn the volume down!

LYDIA: Then I won't be able to hear it.

(Telephone rings)

JAMES: The phone's ringing!

LYDIA: What?

JAMES: The phone is ringing!

LYDIA: What phone?

JAMES: The one you can't hear because the TV is so goddamn loud!—

(He screams bloody murder. Sarah turns back to him)

SARAH: You say something?

JAMES: I screamed. The phone's ringing and the TV's going at about a hundred and ten decibels.

(Buzzer sounds)

Ah, and there's the buzzer on the oven.

(Sarah doesn't understand)

The buzzer on the oven! Now, if someone would fire a bazooka through the window ...

SARAH: What?

JAMES: *(Answering "phone")* Hello!—Would you hold on a minute, please—The buzzer on the oven—your casserole is ready—Hello, yes, I'm listening, you have my undivided attention. Who the hell is this? ... Ask him to wait a second.

(Going to Sarah at the "oven" where her casserole is smoking)

It's for you. It's one of the dorm counselors translating a
call from Che Guevara—

SARAH: Who?

JAMES: Orin. Orin. *Lydia—for crissake!*

LYDIA: *Oh—Okay.*

(Lydia "turns down" the TV)

JAMES: *(Back to "phone" with Sarah in tow)* Hello ... Yes,
Sarah's here. Is Orin there? Are you both ready, because
we're both ready. Okay, this is Sarah speaking to Orin.

SARAH: I don't want to speak to you very much.

JAMES: *(Into "phone")* I don't want to speak to you very
much. *(To Sarah)* Please, I need to see you and Jim. *(Unsigned)* Jim—he's calling me Jim. *(Into "phone")* No,
don't translate that to Orin. I was talking to myself.

(During the exchange above, Lydia slips away)

SARAH: What?

JAMES: *(To Sarah)* Please.

SARAH: You're saying please?

JAMES: No, I'm not saying please. *(Into "phone")* Hold on.
(To Sarah) That was Orin saying please again. My fault—I
probably sounded like me instead of like the dorm
counselor sounding like Orin. Can I help you?

SARAH: I don't want to see him.

JAMES: You don't want to see him—then don't see him. *(Into
"phone")* She doesn't want—

SARAH: Please come for dinner tomorrow night.

JAMES: *(Into "phone")* Please come for dinner tomorrow
night. *(To Sarah)* I would like that. What time should I
come?

SARAH: Seven.

JAMES: *(Into "phone")* Come at seven o'clock. *(To Sarah)*
Good, I'll see you then.

(He slams down the phone. It's quiet)

Hey, either I've just become deaf or it's suddenly quiet in here.

(Music: Bach Double Concerto in D minor, Second Movement, largo ma non tanto. James gets deeply into the music, his eyes closed. Sarah in her own world, but then looking at James, happy to see him serenely involved. The following is in sign language only as she comes and rests her head in his lap)

JAMES: Anytime things get too serious or I don't know how to fix something, I make a joke and that's supposed to make it okay. I didn't know that. In other words, you're saying what? That I obfuscate the truth ... ? How the hell do you sign "obfuscate" *(With resignation, he tries to finger spell)* I [o-b-f-u-s—] *(His fingers lock in a spasm)* My hands are killing me and my brain feels like a slab of ... Look at that—I can't even spell "slab." My brain feels like a slab of ... I'm going to put my hands into a s-a-u-n-a b-a-t-h. Hey—another bad joke! We don't even have one. I'm going to rest my hands and listen to twenty minutes of B-a-c-h. Do you know I haven't turned on my stereo since we got married? Hold it, that sounds like ...

SARAH: Sshh.

JAMES: ... I'm blaming you for the fact I haven't been listening to music.

(James mimes flagellating himself)

SARAH: Sshh. I should give you a day off once a week when you don't have to answer the phone or translate for me or sign to me when we're alone.

JAMES: You should give me a day off once a week when I don't have to answer the phone or translate for you or sign to you when we're alone. That's not what I meant. I was only saying—

SARAH: Sshh. Rest your hands, listen to your music.

JAMES: Rest my hands. Listen to my music.

(Music: Bach Double Concerto in D minor, Second Movement, largo ma non tanto. James gets deeply into the music, his eyes closed. Sarah in her own world, but then looking at James, happy to see him serenely involved. The following is in sign language only as she comes and rests her head in his lap)

SARAH: Enjoying yourself?

JAMES: [Very much. You?]

SARAH: Yes.

JAMES: [What are you doing?]

SARAH: Thinking.

JAMES: [Why don't you read a book?]

SARAH: Why don't *you* read a book?

JAMES: [Because I'm listening to music.]

SARAH: So I'm thinking.

JAMES: [About what?]

SARAH: Sorry. Sshh. Enjoy your music.

(He tries to concentrate on the music. She "busies" herself around the apartment. He can't concentrate, turns off music)

JAMES: *(Speaking and signing again)* I can't.

SARAH: Why not?

JAMES: I can't enjoy my music because you can't.

SARAH: We can enjoy different things.

JAMES: Sure we can enjoy different things; but, in the case of music, you don't have a choice.

SARAH: But I *can* enjoy your music.

JAMES: But you *can* enjoy my music. How?

SARAH: Vibrations.   JAMES: Oh, yeah, vibrations through your nose.

SARAH: Really! The vibrations don't have a sound but they do have a feel.

(She demonstrates)

60

Fast. Slow. Very intense. Not so intense.

JAMES: The vibrations don't have a sound but they do have a feel. Fast and slow ...

SARAH: And when I see people dancing, I feel still more.

JAMES: And when you see people dancing, you feel still more. But you're getting it through them. That's all visual. You're missing *music*.

SARAH: No. I can feel it.

JAMES: I know you can feel it. But that's just a small part of it. You see, music is ... *(Incredible subject to communicate)* Music has a ... *(But he's going to try)* Music starts with pitches. [P-i-t-c-h-e-s.] Sounds! High and low. A whole, huge range of sounds. And each one has its own emotional life. And then when you combine them and play them together—these two and these two—it has a whole *new* life. And then you can play them on different in-struments—trombones, violins, flutes, and drums—The combinations are infinite! And then when you put it all together, with a beginning, a middle, and an end, it grows into a ... It transcends mere sound and speaks directly to your heart—because you *hear* it! I don't have the signs that can ... I can't explain it, I'm sorry.

SARAH: Don't be sorry. I could never know what music sounds like. But just watching you explain to me what you feel, I *can* understand what it means to you. And that makes me very happy.

JAMES: Don't be sorry. You could never know what music sounds like. But just watching me explain what I feel, you *can* understand what it means to me. And that makes you very happy. But it makes me sad for you, damn it!

SARAH: Sshh. No. Don't be, please.

JAMES: Don't be. All right, I'm not. There. Want to take in a vibration or two with me?

(Organ Music: Bach "Toccata and fugue in D minor." James turns the volume way up. They get on the floor together)

[You feel it?]

61

(He tries to demonstrate the first chords of the toccata with his hands, how they rise to crescendo)

SARAH: *(Rising)* I don't like this kind of music.

JAMES: You don't like this kind of music?

SARAH: Organ music.

JAMES: That's right—it is organ music. How did you know it's organ music?

SARAH: I can go in the kitchen.

JAMES: Don't go in the kitchen! Stay here with me and I'll turn it down. *(He does)* What have you got against organ music?

SARAH AND JAMES: *(James translating in the second person)* When we were kids in school here, on Sunday they made us go to church. They played an organ fiercely. Orin cried because he could hear just enough for it to hurt his ears. The kids with hearing aids were forbidden to turn them off. We were told it was the voice of God and should hurt. They said we should love God for being so fierce and demanding. When Orin was nine and I was eleven, we started hiding in the trees behind the duck pond on Sunday. We pretended we were soldiers and threw dirt clods at the church and made sounds like hand grenades.

JAMES: What did they sound like?

SARAH: No.

JAMES: C'mon. You show me a deaf guy's hand grenade and I'll stop playing my organ so fiercely.

(Orin enters. He and Sarah mime "explosion" of a hand grenade, only Orin making a small sound)

ORIN: You remember that? That was our first rebellion. We were a really good team.

SARAH: How do you like my apartment?

ORIN: Your apartment is very nice.

JAMES: You're speaking much better, Orin.

ORIN: Thank you. I've been working very hard at it. *(To Sarah)* I want to—

62

SARAH: Come see my kitchen.

ORIN: I'll see your kitchen later. I need to—

SARAH: Come.

(She moves to "kitchen")

ORIN: *(Following)* Excuse me, Jim.

JAMES: Sure.

SARAH: Look at this machine. It does eleven things.

ORIN: A machine. It does eleven things.

SARAH: *(Demonstrates)* It stirs, chops, beats, grates, mixes, grinds, crumbs, shakes, blends, purees, and liquefies.

(She "pours" it into a "glass," hands it to Orin)

ORIN: My mother has a blender too, Sarah. Now, can I tell you what I have to tell you—even though you don't want to hear it.

SARAH: We weren't really a good team.

ORIN: What do you mean, we weren't really a good team? We were friends. More than that—we were brother and sister.

SARAH: True, but I was never good at the kind of rebellion you wanted. But I am starting to feel I'm good at this. And happy.

ORIN: But you were never good at the kind of rebellion I wanted. But you are starting to feel you're good at this. And you're happy. I can see that. But we really need you across the street.

JAMES: May I come in? What is it you need her *for*, Orin?

KLEIN: *(Entering)* Dear Mr. Dennis, I must confess, I never thought about discrimination against the deaf. I think you might have a legitimate complaint with the Equal Employment Opportunity Commission.

SARAH: A complaint?

JAMES: You're gonna file a complaint*!*

ORIN: Damn right.

KLEIN: Hiring practices are definitely open to question in your institution.

ORIN: Which is supposed to exist for our benefit.

KLEIN: Let me know if this is an arena you and Miss Norman would like to enter.

(Klein goes)

ORIN: *(To Sarah)* I want you with me.

SARAH: With you? Or to follow you?

ORIN: Not to follow me. With me.

SARAH: Why?

ORIN: Because you're deaf. And pure deaf.   And because you're as strong as I am. Or you were.

SARAH: I'm not interested. I'm trying to do other things.

ORIN: You're not interested. You're trying to do other things. But you can't go from closing yourself in the school with your brooms and mops to closing yourself in here with your TV and your blender.

SARAH: I'm not closed in here! It's not the same!

ORIN: You're not closed in here—it's not the same! What's the difference?

SARAH: Are you kidding?

ORIN: No, I'm not kidding!

SARAH: A world of difference!

ORIN: A world of difference! Listen, I didn't come here to start a fight.

JAMES: Orin, Orin, hold it!

SARAH: You have a lot of gall! Big-headed!

JAMES: Orin, excuse me for being here, but I have been cast in the role of Sarah's mentor, so lay off her, huh.

SARAH: What are you saying?

JAMES: Nothing. Between Orin and me.

SARAH: But about me.

64

ORIN: He's trying to protect you from me.

SARAH: Neither of you has to protect me from anyone.

JAMES AND ORIN: That's right, she doesn't need either one of us to protect her from ...

(They look at each other, stop in mid-sentence)

ORIN: Please, at least meet the lawyer. Read the research. Here.

SARAH: Maybe.

ORIN: Read it.

SARAH: Put it down.

(He puts it down)

ORIN: We need your help too, Jim. Will you stand with us?

JAMES: What would you want me to do?

ORIN: We'll need someone who hears and speaks to make phone calls for us for several weeks.

JAMES: Phone calls. For several weeks.

ORIN: We'll need a translator. You'll speak as if you're me—

JAMES: Oh, I know the routine. I'm already Mrs. Leeds' social secretary. You're sure you haven't got anything important I could do—something with a prefix in front of it maybe—Captain, Lord ...

ORIN: ˙ I need someone who isn't afraid of a fight ... or of a little competition.

(A beat)

JAMES: I see. Excuse me. *(To Sarah, who is glancing at the research)* If you're interested, I'm interested.

ORIN: Sarah, please don't turn away from us.

(Sarah and Orin launch into an untranslated, *totally silent argument in ASL that is beyond James' ability to keep up. A translation is printed opposite)*

SARAH: *(ASL)* You dirty business.

SARAH: This is a dirty thing to do.

ORIN: We need you.

ORIN: We need you.

SARAH: You never share.

SARAH: You won't share.

ORIN: ? You-two share? "y" sweet romance last Doubt Deaf rights beat!

ORIN: Does he share with you? Do you think this little romance will last half as long as what we can accomplish for our people?

JAMES: What?

SARAH: You big-headed talk that.

SARAH: You have no right to say that!

ORIN: Me big-head? We-two discuss plan, will do 1-2-3-4. Thrill change?

ORIN: What do you mean I have no right? We've discussed it. Planned all these things to do. Why have you changed?

SARAH: We-two never discuss.

SARAH: We never discussed anything.

ORIN: Bullshit. We-two finish talk. We-two deaf. Don't forget. We-two deaf! Period!

ORIN: Bullshit. We've already discussed it. We're deaf. Don't forget it. You and I are deaf! Period!

ORIN: *(Speaking to James)* Good night, Jim. I'll be in touch with you.

JAMES: Yeah, Fine. Sure.

(Orin leaves)

I feel like everyone was talking in some far-northern dialect of Hungarian there. What was that all about?

SARAH: Between Orin and me.

JAMES: Between Orin and you. Hey, whudduya know, I don't like being closed out either. What was that I caught there about a "romance."

SARAH: He said our marriage won't last. It isn't as important as deaf rights.

JAMES: He said our marriage won't last. It isn't as important as deaf rights. Really. What did you say?

SARAH: He practically accused me of being a phony hearing person.

JAMES: He practically accused you of being a phony hearing person. My God, the worst insult possible. You know what he's trying to do, don't you? It's the oldest trick in the repressed-minority handbook. He wants you to feel guilty for leaving the flock.

SARAH: I haven't left the deaf world. I haven't done anything yet.

JAMES: You haven't left the deaf world. You haven't done anything yet. Hey, hey, sit down. What you and I have to do is separate the fact that he may have a legitimate axe to grind from the fact that he's a rotten little shit.

SARAH: No more words tonight. I'm too confused and angry.

JAMES: No more words tonight. You're too confused and angry. You think silence is the best thing for confusion and anger?

SARAH: It's not silent in my head.

JAMES: It's not silent in your head. Hey, we're a team, remember? You're not the only one he insulted. I don't like being minimized any more than you do.

SARAH: What's going on between Orin and me is not about your ego.

JAMES: What's going on between Orin and you is not about my ...

(Sarah moves off to one side)

... ego.

(Miss Klein, with a note)

KLEIN: *(To Orin, as he enters, carefully articulating and speaking a bit loudly)*

Excuse me. Do ... you ... know ... where ... this ... is?

ORIN: Miss Klein?

KLEIN: Yes.

ORIN: I'm Orin Dennis.

KLEIN: Oh—Orin! Hello. Finally. I had a little difficulty finding the building.

ORIN: You found it. Come on in, please. This is Sarah Norman.

SARAH: Leeds.

ORIN: Sarah Leeds—I'm sorry. Edna Klein.

KLEIN: *(Articulating carefully, a bit loudly)* Hello, Sarah, I'm so pleased to meet you finally.

(Orin translates Miss Klein's words for Sarah throughout this scene)

SARAH: Thank you.

ORIN: She said, thank you.

KLEIN: *(Picking up the sign)* Thank you? *(Speaking only)* Now then, I'm to speak directly into your faces, is that right?

ORIN: My face. She doesn't lip read. Can you understand me okay?

KLEIN: Yes. Yes, I can.

SARAH: My husband James.

(James is perusing the research)

ORIN: Sarah's husband James. One of our team.

KLEIN: *(Into his face)* I'm so pleased to meet you finally.

JAMES: *(Imitating Klein's precision and loudness)* Thank you. I am so pleased to meet you, too. Finally.

ORIN: I don't think that's very funny, Jim.

KLEIN: Am I missing some-   SARAH: *(To Orin)* What's he
thing?   doing?

JAMES: I can hear.

68

KLEIN: Excuse me ... ?   ORIN: [He's pretending to be deaf.]

JAMES: I'm a hearing person. You don't have to speak directly into my face or raise your voice.

KLEIN: Was I talking loudly?

JAMES: A natural mistake.

KLEIN: *(With her back to Sarah and Orin)* I was so sure I was going to handle this flawlessly that I suppose there was no alternative but to make an immediate fool of myself. I'm sorry.

JAMES: Forget it.   SARAH: *(To Orin)* What are they saying?

ORIN: What is she saying?

JAMES: Nothing. I just told her I'm not deaf.

ORIN: He is a hearing person, Miss Klein. He was just making a joke.

JAMES: Yeah, I just told—

KLEIN: Yes, he told me.

JAMES: *(To Sarah, who isn't pleased)* Sorry.

KLEIN: Well, could we, uh ...

(Sarah gestures for them to sit)

So, this is the young woman you wrote me about, Orin. Sarah.

SARAH: *(To Klein)* He shouldn't have used my name without permission—

ORIN: *(Ignoring Sarah's line above)* Sarah, yes.

KLEIN: As I understand it, Sarah is deaf *and* dumb.

(James makes the sound of a bomb going off)

SARAH: I'm not deaf and
dumb. I'm—

ORIN: We don't like the word
"dumb" very much,
Miss Klein. We are deaf
or hearing impaired and
we speak or we don't
speak.

KLEIN: Of course. Excuse me. Sarah is deaf and doesn't speak.

SARAH: Yes. That's what I was trying to say.

(Orin ignores Sarah)

KLEIN: Well, unhappy as that may have made you all your life,
it could be very useful to you now.

SARAH: I'm not unhappy—

ORIN: She's not unhappy being deaf, Miss Klein, that's not the
point. What she means is that she is often misunderstood
by hearing people. She wants—

(Angry at Orin speaking for her, Sarah moves away)

I'm sorry. I didn't mean to speak for you. I just—

SARAH: But you did!

(Orin goes)

KLEIN: Look, I'm sorry I appear to be so ... Mr. Leeds,
you tell her I'll do better next time.

JAMES: Right, yes, I will, I will.

(Klein goes)

Fun evening. I thought the charades went particularly well.

SARAH: I think Klein is going to be very good.

JAMES: You think Klein is going to be very good at what?

SARAH: You were being so cute together I thought you
liked her.

JAMES: We were being so cute together you thought I liked
her. Why would I like her?

70

SARAH: She can hear and she's educated.

JAMES: She can hear, she's educated. Oh, come on, if you'd stop pretending to be deaf and listen to her, you'd know she has the remains of a bilateral lisp. *(Imitating a bilateral lisp)* She probably sounded like this before speech therapy ... You have no reason to be jealous of her. Am I jealous of Orin?

SARAH: Maybe.

JAMES: Maybe? Hey, I don't know which role you're playing here. Is this Sarah the Pure Deaf Person, or Sarah Norman, the old isolationist maid, or is this Sarah Leeds, teammate of James? What's eating you?

SARAH: Let's go to sleep.

JAMES: No, I don't want to go to bed. You can't just start a bonfire in the living room and then go night-night. Here, let's talk.

(He sits)

SARAH: I can't.

JAMES: You can't.

(She goes to the "bedroom." He follows)

That's great. You be deaf, I'll be mute, and we'll burn our eyes out with the fire in the living room, then pray for arthritis. Not bad, huh? No hear, no speak, no see, no hands. Oh, Sarah, Sarah, let's crawl under the covers and pretend we're in a faraway place.

SARAH: We're not. We're here.

JAMES: We're not. We're here. All right, then, deal with what's bothering you!

SARAH: I don't know which role I'm supposed to play. Orin treats me like an idiot. You treat me like an idiot. Now the lady lawyer treats me like an idiot.

JAMES: You don't know which role you're supposed to play. Orin treats you like an idiot. I treat you like an idiot. Now

71

the lady lawyer treats you—Wait a second, I don't treat you like an idiot.

SARAH: Let me be a person.

JAMES: I don't want you to be a person?

SARAH: You want me to be a *deaf* person so you can change me into a hearing person.

JAMES: I want you to be a *deaf* person so I can change you into a hearing person.

(He moves away)

Good night.

SARAH: *(Getting his attention)* Orin doesn't want me to be a hearing person because he needs a pure deaf person.

JAMES: Orin doesn't want you to be a hearing person because he needs a pure deaf person.

SARAH: And the lady lawyer wants me to hate being deaf so all the hearing people will feel sorry for me.

JAMES: And the lady lawyer wants you to hate being deaf so all the hearing people will feel sorry for you.

SARAH: And I just want to be me.

JAMES: And you just want to be you. And who are you?

(On Sarah's face we see confusion. She doesn't have an answer)

Oh, Christ. How did we go from being Ozzie and Harriet to—

(He tries to embrace her. She pushes him away)

SARAH: Don't pity me.

JAMES: Don't pity you. Wait a minute! I may be just a middle-class, white, Jewish-Catholic atheist, hearing person, but I have rights too. And one of those rights is to feel sympathy for my wife even if she's an inordinate hard ass. And I don't know the sign for inordinate but I don't care. Here's "hard ass" — it's a beauty!

72

(He makes to lower his pants. Sarah "turns the lights out."

In the dark, the sound of Sarah crying softly. James "turns the lights on" again)

I never heard you cry before.

SARAH: I wasn't crying.

JAMES: Yes you were. I know because I heard you. See, we don't have to look at each other or even touch to communicate ... Let's go back to being alone together. Let's have a baby.

SARAH: A baby?

JAMES: Yes.

SARAH: No. If it were deaf, you would hate it.

JAMES: If it were deaf, I would hate it. That's a goddamn lie! If it were deaf and grew up to be as unbending as its mother, though—

(She "turns out the lights" again)

Goddamnit!

(Music: A Handel oratorio. Lights. James listening to his stereo)

KLEIN: *(Entering)* Good evening, Mr. Leeds. Are Orin and Sarah here yet?

JAMES: Huh?

KLEIN: *(Speaking over the music)* Are Orin and Sarah here yet?

JAMES: Orin is here. Sarah is not. But I really wouldn't count on her continued participation in this ... whatever it is.

KLEIN: Oh, I hope you're mistaken.

JAMES: I am never mistaken, Miss Klein—it's my saving grace.

KLEIN: You're very fortunate.

JAMES: Yes, I am, thank you.

KLEIN: Can I show you what I learned today and you tell me if I'm doing it right?

JAMES: Sure. What have you learned?

(She puts down her briefcase)

Don't tell me: I'll bet you've learned some Signed English, haven't you, so you can communicate with our deaf brothers and sisters.

KLEIN: Well, I've made a start. Could we turn the Handel off, please?

JAMES: Handel?

KLEIN: I'm sorry, I thought you were listening to Handel.

JAMES: Oh, I am.

KLEIN: Oh, I thought so.

JAMES: Yes, I recall you even said so.

(Music out)

Now.

KLEIN: How. Are. You?

JAMES: I am fine, Miss Klein. How are you?

KLEIN: Okay, I think I've got that, too. I. Am. Fine.

JAMES: You want to watch the thumb under the chin. That means "*not*." I'm *not* fine. If you're fine, you want to do "*am*" which is the letter "A," thumb under the lip ...

(He demonstrates. Sarah has seen part of this. Klein discovers her watching)

KLEIN: Your wife. Hello, Sarah.

SARAH: *(To James)* More cuteness.

JAMES: More cuteness? Where were you when I got up this morning?

KLEIN: Would you like me to wait outside?

JAMES: That's quite all right.

SARAH: What did she say?

JAMES: She wants to know if we want her to wait outside while we do our husband and wife routine.

74

KLEIN: Sarah, Mr. Leeds suggested you might be considering dropping out of our—

SARAH: What did she say now?

JAMES: I don't feel like telling you what she's saying. You've been gone all day—where have you been?

ORIN: *(Entering)* Sarah, where have you been? Hello, Miss Klein.

KLEIN: Hello.

ORIN: I wanted you to be with me when I told Franklin.

FRANKLIN: *(Entering; apart from the scene)* I think my hearing aid just blew up in my ear. You and Sarah are going to do what?

ORIN: And I wanted you to read Miss Klein's speech before she got here.

SARAH: *(Snatching the speech)* I've got it. I'll read it.

FRANKLIN: Ask Mr. Leeds to come see me.

ORIN: Where did you go?

FRANKLIN: Tell him to see me.

(Franklin exits)

KLEIN: Orin, tell Sarah I want to say something to her.

(Orin taps Sarah's shoulder. She looks up)

How. Are. You?

SARAH: Lousy.

ORIN: She's a bit perturbed, Miss Klein. How are you?

KLEIN: I. Am. Fine. Thank you.

(Sarah and Orin less than knocked out)

JAMES: They're bowled over, Miss Klein.

(Orin turns his attention to Sarah's perusal of Klein's speech)

ORIN: *(ASL only)* [Just read it.]

KLEIN: Okay. Okay. I don't suppose that either you or they came equipped with a complete vocabulary or dancing fingers either.

JAMES: Whatever you do, Miss Klein, don't accuse them of any imperfections.

KLEIN: *(Waves for their attention)* Orin? Sarah? What do you think of my remarks for the commission?

SARAH: Same old shit.

(James laughs)

KLEIN: *(To Orin)* What did she say?

ORIN: Nothing. She thinks they're—

SARAH: *(To Orin)* Tell her.

ORIN: Sarah, what's your problem?

KLEIN: *(To James)* What's the matter? What did Sarah say, Mr. Leeds?

JAMES: Come here, I'll tell you.

ORIN: Stay out of this, Jim.

JAMES: All right.

ORIN: The speech, Miss Klein, is okay, but it's basically what hearing people always say. We do not consider ourselves helpless in any way.

JAMES: Could I interrupt, please? Miss Klein, why don't you just let them do it themselves?

KLEIN: What do you mean? Walk out on them?

JAMES: No, sit here and give them whatever legal expertise you can but let them speak for themselves.

KLEIN: *(Excluding Orin and Sarah)* I'm not sure that would be quite as impressive as—

JAMES: Impressive!

KLEIN: Just a minute! I had planned to call on them to answer some questions—

JAMES: Excuse me, Orin has his hand raised.

76

ORIN: If you don't mind, Miss Klein, I would like to participate in any discussion you're having that will affect me.

JAMES: She's saying that you, with your hard-won speaking ability, and Sarah the Pure Deaf person are going to sit silently by looking properly pathetic while Miss Klein makes your case for you.

KLEIN: Mr. Leeds, I'm perfectly capable of speaking for my-self, thank you.

SARAH: Here are the two hearing people arguing while we stand and wait for you to decide what will be done *for* us.

JAMES: *(As Sarah signs)* My wife has both her hands up now.

KLEIN: What? What is the difficulty?

ORIN: Nothing.

SARAH: *(To James)* Tell her what I said.

JAMES: She said, Here are the two hearing people arguing while the two deaf people stand around and wonder what is to be decided *for* them.

SARAH: Same old shit.

JAMES: Same old shit.

KLEIN: So that's what it means. I see.

SARAH: Just like your speech.

JAMES: Just like your speech.

KLEIN: Yeah, I got that, thank you.

JAMES: Good, then you don't need me.

ORIN: Maybe we could suggest a few changes in your speech.

KLEIN: Yes, I think it's time you do the talking and I do the listening.

SARAH: She won't listen.

ORIN: How do you know she won't listen?

SARAH: Because none of them do!

ORIN: You can't just stand around and be cynical. That's what you've done all your life. Don't you want to do something for yourself besides spit on the deaf world and lick the ass of the hearing world?

JAMES: Hey!

SARAH: Yes.

ORIN: So, help us.

JAMES: Hey, Orin, you know talk like that doesn't make things any easier around here. *You know?*

ORIN: Making things easier for you, Jim, isn't one of my first concerns just now. *(To Sarah)* Now, are you going to help us or not? If not, I've had enough of you.

JAMES: She's not interested! Tell them you're not interested and let's get them the hell out of our home.

SARAH: Each of you keeps making me feel—bow down.

JAMES: Each of us keeps making you feel ... What's that? "Bow down"?

ORIN: That she owes us something.

ORIN: What?   JAMES: What?

SARAH: I don't know!

ORIN: *(To Klein)* She   JAMES: You don't know.
doesn't know.

SARAH: But I'm not sitting here and letting you talk about me! Who I owe something to is *me*! I want something said about *me*.

ORIN: But she's not going to sit there and let us talk about ...

JAMES: But you're not going to sit there—*(To Orin)* Take it.

ORIN: Who she owes something to is her. She wants something said about her. Good.

KLEIN. *(As Orin reverses to Sarah)* Fine. Tell her we'll sit down and I'll write something about her.

SARAH: No! No more. I'll say it myself.

ORIN: No! No more. She will say—

(He stops himself from speaking out loud what she said)

SARAH: And I'll write it myself!

ORIN: *(Signing only)* [What are you talking about?]

SARAH: Tell her that!

ORIN: *(Signing and speaking)* I'm not telling her that because you're not going to do that!

KLEIN: What is she saying? SARAH: *(To James)* Tell her what I said!

ORIN: *(To James)* Don't translate!

JAMES: Sarah wants to make her own speech. One that she will write herself.

SARAH: *(To Orin and Klein)* And neither of you has anything to say about what I write.

JAMES: Neither of you has anything to say about what she writes.

SARAH: That's it—take it or leave it.

JAMES: That's it—take it or leave it.

KLEIN: *(Gathering her things)* Well, as I'm obviously not loaded with expertise, I guess I should gratefully take it. How do you sign "terrific"?

JAMES: *(Signing)* [Terrific.]

KLEIN: *(Holding her coat and briefcase under her arm so she can do the two-handed sign)* Terrific.

SARAH: Thank you.

ORIN: I'll write my own speech too, then.

SARAH: That's up to you. Nobody's going to speak for me anymore. Tell her that.

JAMES: No one is ever going to speak for Sarah again.

(Klein and Orin recede and exit)

SARAH: Did you hear yourself say that?

JAMES: Yes, I heard myself repeat that. What I'm a bit confused about is how we got here. Lemme see if I've got this straight. We met, we fought, we fell in love, we got married, I was happy, I thought you were happy. Now we're kicking each other's teeth in. Explain it to me.

SARAH: You think it's my fault and that you're perfect.

JAMES: I think it's your fault and that I'm perfect. What a crock of ...

(She goes to another area of the stage to work on her speech)

LYDIA: *(Entering)* Hello, Mr. Leeds, where's Sarah?

JAMES: I don't know.

(Sarah, writing her speech, very into it)

LYDIA: She's at the duck pond—I just saw her. She told me to leave her alone. So I did. Everybody says you're giving Sarah back to the school, that you don't want her anymore.

JAMES: Everybody's saying what?

LYDIA: Yup. And frankly, I think that's a wise con ... con-tem-pla-tion. Boy, I'm thirsty.

JAMES: Okay, one quick drink and then off you go. No TV tonight. What would you like?

LYDIA: You got a beer?

JAMES: How 'bout a beer?

LYDIA: Okay. Boy, it sure is hot, isn't it?

(She begins to fan with the top of her blouse, exposing just a glimpse of breast)

JAMES: Oh Lydia, for Chrissake, why aren't you wearing a bra?

LYDIA: A what?

JAMES: A bra.

LYDIA: Oh ... I forgot. Oh no.

JAMES: I think we'd better get something straight about our relationship, you and I—

LYDIA: Here it is!

(She pulls the bra from her pants pocket)

JAMES: No. No. No. Lydia, listen to me ...

LYDIA: I'm sorry. Don't embarrass me, please. I'll just leave.

(Lydia runs off. James moves after Lydia a step or two; then to Sarah at the "duck pond")

JAMES: Working on your speech, huh?

SARAH: Yes.

JAMES: I'm through with my classes. Can I help you?

SARAH: Thanks, no.

JAMES: Throw in a few jokes?

SARAH: You're not funny in deaf, only in hearing.

JAMES: I'm not funny in deaf, only in hearing. See you at home?

SARAH: Few minutes.

(She turns her attention back to her writing)

FRANKLIN: *(Entering)* Make a settlement with them!

JAMES: Yes!

FRANKLIN: They've got as much chance of—

JAMES: Aw, come on, you could make a settlement with them and they'd never have to go in front of that damned commission. A lot of embarrassment could be avoided.

FRANKLIN: The only people who're gonna be embarrassed are your wife and our friend Orin.

JAMES: Well, couldn't you spare them that?

FRANKLIN: Lemme explain the facts of life to you, James. The commission will find in their favor; they always find in favor of the downtrodden. Why not? They know they haven't got an ounce of legal power. They're merely one of those liberal showcase apparatus whose opinion no one is bound to abide by. I'll make your wife and our friend Orin take me into court. If they win there, I'll appeal. I'll make them fight me for years.

JAMES: Why?

81

FRANKLIN: Because, despicable as it may seem, I won't continue in this field if the subjects of my efforts are going to tell me how to minister to them. Look, Orin is potentially a fine teacher—he has all the communication skills—but he's a rarity. Would you hire your wife to teach? What—sign? That'd be like a football team hiring a guy to do nothing but hold for extra points.

(A beat)

All right, I'll make a settlement, Jimbo.

(James, with Franklin, watching Sarah)

JAMES: What did you say?

FRANKLIN: I'll make you a hero. Tell them I'll agree to hire a new deaf gym teacher and deaf dietician. Offer them that.

JAMES: That won't be enough.

FRANKLIN: You want to know a secret? Nothing would be. Nothing would be enough.

(He exits)

JAMES: *(To Sarah)* You're home from work.

SARAH: It's exciting to feel I have a job.

JAMES: It's exciting to feel you have a job. Good. I'm glad.

SARAH: Are you?

JAMES: Trying to be.

SARAH: Would you watch me practice my speech?

JAMES: Sure, I'd like to watch you practice your speech.

SARAH: But don't tell me how to make it better.

JAMES: But don't tell you how to make it better. What do you mean, don't criticize it?

SARAH: Right.

JAMES: What if your English is incorrect and I think the commission people won't understand it.

SARAH: You can tell me that.

JAMES: I can tell you that—thank you. Will you want me to translate as if I'm you?

SARAH: What do you mean?

JAMES: I mean, when we go before the commission—do you want me to translate the speech exactly—

SARAH: Do you think you're going to translate for me?

JAMES: Yes, I assumed I'd translate for you. I'll tell you a little secret. They won't understand it if I don't translate it.

SARAH: I want Orin to do it.

JAMES: You want Orin to do it? Why? Because he's hearing impaired? So you're gonna turn the tables now, and start using Orin, huh?

(A beat)

Look, I'd like to be your translator. If you're really going to go through with this I'd like to share the experience with you.

SARAH: I can't say what I feel about being deaf through a hearing person.

JAMES: You can't say what you feel about being deaf through ... through a hearing person.

SARAH: Does that make you angry?

JAMES: Yes, that makes me angry!

SARAH: And hurt?

JAMES: And hurt ... ? Let me see the speech, okay? Show me.

(He translates as if he were she)

SARAH AND JAMES: My name is Sarah Norman Leeds, a name I wrote with my fingers faster than you can say it with your mouth. So I will not be keeping you any longer than I would if I were speaking or if, as always is the way, somebody else were speaking for me.

(He finishes some distance behind her)

.s: Good. That's very good.

.AH AND JAMES: For all my life I have been the creation of other people. The first thing I was ever able to understand was that everyone was supposed to hear but I couldn't and that was bad. Then they told me everyone was supposed to be smart but I was dumb. Then they said, oh no, I wasn't permanently dumb, only temporarily, but to be smart I had to become an imitation of the people who had from birth everything a person has to have to be good: ears that hear, mouth that speaks, eyes that read, brain that understands. Well, my brain understands a lot; and my eyes are my ears; and my hands are my voice; and my language, my speech, my ability to communicate is as great as yours. Greater, maybe, because I can communicate to you in one image an idea more complex than you can speak to each other in fifty words. For example, the sign "to connect," a simple sign—but it means so much more when it is moved between us like this. Now it means to be joined in a shared relationship, to be individual yet as one. A whole concept just like that. Well, I want to be joined to other people, but for all my life people have spoken for me: *She* says; *she* means; *she* wants. As if there were no I. As if there were no one in here who *could* understand. Until you let me be an individual, an *I*, just as you are, you will never truly be able to come inside my silence and know me. And until you can do that, I will never let myself know you. Until that time, we cannot be joined. We cannot share a relationship.

(Silence)

JAMES: Well, you ... That's all very ... That's moving—it is, but ...

SARAH: But you're pitying me.

JAMES: But I'm pitying you? Is that it? Is that it? That I'm pitying you? Maybe it is. You ... You certainly unloaded a few of your favorite ... You think they're really ... that *we're* really going to—we insensitive and inarticulate hearing people—that we're really going to be able to—that one out of a million is going to care enough to even *try* to come inside your silence, to bend to you ... Look, Sarah, I went to see Franklin today. I tried to get him to make a settlement with Orin—Excuse me, I should say Orin and you now, shouldn't I? I tried to save you the frustration of going before that group of hearing men who spend their lives listening to minorities vent their anger against the majority—and you know what he said?

SARAH: You tried to get him to make a settlement?

JAMES: I tried ... Exactly right! I want to save you—

SARAH: After telling Klein to let us speak for ourselves, you went to Franklin to—

JAMES: After telling Klein to let you speak for yourselves— Hey, just a second, you're my wife—it's not like—

SARAH: Not like what? Didn't you listen to anything I just said?

JAMES: Yes I did. Yes I did, I heard every word you just said and I'm going to tell you something you're not gonna like.

SARAH: Give it to me!

JAMES: I think your real bitch—yours and Orin's—is that you are deaf and you wish you could hear.

SARAH: You didn't hear a word I said.

JAMES: I just said I heard every goddamn word you said. I also just said I think you're lying. I don't think you think being deaf is so goddamn wonderful.

SARAH: Because of people like you.

JAMES: No! Not because of people like me! Franklin, the administrators in ninety percent of the schools in the country, would never hire you. You're dreaming a dream that can't come true.

SARAH: Then I won't be a teacher.

JAMES: Then you won't be a teacher. Okay, what will you be?

SARAH: I'll go in the street with the little manual alphabet cards and beg for money.

JAMES: You'll go in the street with the little manual alphabet cards and beg for money. That's perfect!

SARAH: Or I'll be your maid.

JAMES: Or you'll be my maid. Right. And we'll have deaf children.

SARAH: Right!

JAMES: Who's going to educate them? You?

SARAH: Better me than you.

JAMES: Yeah? You think I'm going to let you change my children into people like you who so cleverly see vanity and cowardice as pride? You're going nowhere, you're achieving nothing, you're changing nothing until you change.

SARAH: Until I speak!

JAMES: Until you speak—Okay, you wanna play that one—fine with me. Goddamn right! You want to be independent of me, you want to be a person in your own right, you want people not to pity you, but you want them to understand you in the very poetic way you describe in your speech as well as the plain old, boring way *normal* people understand each other, then you learn to read my lips and you learn to use that little mouth of yours for something besides eating and showing me you're better than hearing girls in bed! Come on! Read my lips! What am I saying? Say what I'm saying! What. Am. I. Saying?

(Sarah starts to sign something. He pins her arms. The rest of this is unsigned)

Shut up! You want to talk to me, then *you* learn *my* language! Did you get that? Of course you did. You've probably been reading lips perfectly for years; but it's a great control game, isn't it? You can cook, but you can't speak. You can drive and shop and play bridge but you can't speak. You can even make a speech but you still can't do it alone. You always have to be dependent on someone, and you always will for the rest of your life until you learn to speak. Now come on! I want you to speak to me. Let me hear it. Speak! Speak! Speak!

(She erupts like a volcano in speech. She doesn't sign)

Speech! Speech! Is that it? No! You want me to be your child! You want me to be like you. How do you like my voice? Am I beautiful? Am I what you want me to be? *What about me? What I want? What I want!*

(She can't be sure how this sounds except by his reaction to it. It is clearly sentences, the sense of it intelligible, but it is not a positive demonstration of speech—only of passion. Only a few words are even barely understandable. She sees this in his face, knows for sure now that she does speak as badly as she has supposed she does.

Silence. Close by each other. James reaches to touch her. She bolts away. They're in the same positions they were at the beginning of the play)

Me have nothing. Me deafy. Speech inept. Intelligence—tiny blockhead. English—blow away. Left one you. Depend—no. Think myself enough. Join. Unjoined.

(She goes, but does not leave the stage. James puts his mufflers on, is alone in some silence inside there)

ORIN: *(Entering)* Where's Sarah, Jim? It's time to go.

KLEIN: *(Entering)* Mr. Leeds, the commission is waiting. Can we move along?

ORIN: You're not going to keep her from going, Jim.

KLEIN: Mr. Leeds, are you listening?

ORIN: Jim!

MRS. NORMAN: *(Entering)* Hello, Sarah. Are you all right? How did you get here?

KLEIN: We'll have to go.

ORIN: You haven't heard the last of this, Jim. You hear me?

(They both exit)

MRS. NORMAN: Are you alone?

SARAH: Yes.

87

MRS. NORMAN: Do you want to talk?

SARAH: No.

(Sarah and her mother embrace)

LYDIA: *(Entering)* Hello, Mr. Leeds. Here I am.

(A beat)

> Are you okay? Where's Sarah? Mr. Leeds, everybody says
> Sarah went away. But she didn't, did she? She's really
> here, isn't she? Hiding, huh? Like over there? Nope.
> Maybe over here. Nope. I wonder where she is, Jim.

*(She lets "Jim" hang out there a moment. When she isn't struck
by lightning:)*

> Jimmy.

(A beat. She touches him)

> You need a girl that doesn't go away. You need a girl that
> talks.

*(He takes her hands, pins them together with one hand, puts his
other over her mouth)*

> Someone who loves—

(He presses harder)

> I—

(He presses. She's silent. They look at each other)

MRS. NORMAN: Hello, James.

KLEIN: *(Entering)* We won, Mr. Leeds.

FRANKLIN: *(Entering)* Won? Won what?

ORIN: *(Entering)* We didn't need you and we didn't need
Sarah.

FRANKLIN: Don't you understand? You've won nothing.

KLEIN: *(To James)* Maybe I could buy you lunch someday. Perhaps if we tried talking to each other like two civilized human beings ...

(James puts his mufflers on Klein's head and turns to Mrs. Norman)

JAMES: She's actually here, isn't she, Mrs. Norman? May I see her, please?

MRS. NORMAN: What if she doesn't want to see you?

JAMES: She'll have to tell me. *(To Sarah)* Hello.

MRS. NORMAN: *(To Sarah)* Would you like me to leave you alone?

JAMES: What do you think I'm going to do if you won't talk to me—exit peaceably, leaving you one of my famous notes: "Now that I actually understand *something*, I quit. James Leeds."

SARAH: *(To her mother)* Please.

(Mrs. Norman goes, as do the others)

JAMES: What I did to you last night was ... I need help. Help me.

SARAH: How can I help you?

JAMES: Teach me.

SARAH: You're the teacher.

JAMES: Yes, I'm a terrific teacher: Grow, Sarah, but not too much. Understand yourself, but not better than I understand you. Be brave, but not so brave you don't need me anymore. Your silence frightens me. When I'm in that silence, I hear nothing, I feel like nothing. I can never pull you into my world of sound any more than you can open some magic door and bring me into your silence. I can say that now.

SARAH: And I can say I hurt and know I won't shrivel up and blow away.

JAMES: And you can say you hurt and you know you won't ...

(A beat)

Come home with me.

SARAH: No.

JAMES: Why?

SARAH: I'm afraid I would just go on trying to change you. We would have to meet in another place; not in silence or in sound but somewhere else. I don't know where that is now. I have to go it alone.

JAMES: You're afraid you would just go on trying to change me. We would have to meet in another place; not in silence or in sound but somewhere else. You don't know where that is now. You have to go it alone.

(A beat)

But you will think about trying again with me?

(A beat)

SARAH: Yes. Because no matter who I am, someone inside me loves you very much.

JAMES: Yes, because no matter who you are, someone inside you ... Well, damn it, I love you too.

SARAH: Something else.

JAMES: Something else—What?

SARAH: I don't want deaf children.

JAMES: You don't want deaf children. I'm sorry if I—

SARAH: No. I just don't have the right to demand that anyone be created in my image.

JAMES: You just don't have the right to demand that anyone be created in your image. [Me too.]

(They come together, embrace. She breaks, runs off. James alone)

(Signing and speaking) I think ... I dream ... And in my dream, I see her coming back to me with one last note—this one, though, not one I've written her, summoning her before me, but one she has written me.

(Sarah returns behind James)

It is written in space with her two hands. It says:

JAMES AND SARAH: I'll help you if you'll help me.

SARAH: Join.

(The two of them alone, James turning to her in the fading light)